Political Campaigning and Communication

Series Editor
Darren G. Lilleker, Bournemouth University, Bournemouth, UK

The series explores themes relating to how political organisations promote themselves and how citizens interpret and respond to their tactics. Politics is here defined broadly as any activities designed to have an impact on public policy. The scope of the series thus covers election campaigns, as well as pressure group campaigns, lobbying, and campaigns instigated by social and citizen movements.

Research included in the series might focus on the latest strategies and tactics within political marketing and campaigning, covering topics such as the strategic use of legacy, digital and social media, the use of big data and analytics for targeting citizens, and the use of manipulative tactics and disinformation.

Furthermore, as campaigns are an important interface between the institutions of power and citizens, they present opportunities to examine their impact in engaging, involving and mobilizing citizens. Areas of focus might include attitudes and voting behavior, political polarization and the campaign environment, public discourse around campaigns, and the psychologies underpinning civil society and protest movements.

Works may take a narrow or broad perspective. Single-nation case studies of one specific campaign and comparative cross-national or temporal studies are equally welcome. The series also welcomes themed edited collections which explore a central set of research questions.

For an informal discussion for a book in the series, please contact the series editor Darren Lilleker (dlilleker@bournemouth.ac.uk), or Ambra Finotello (ambra.finotello@palgrave.com).

This book series is indexed by Scopus.

Fouad Touzani

Marketing US Foreign Policy in the MENA Region

American Presidents vs Non-State Actors

Fouad Touzani
Sidi Mohamed Ben Abdullah
University
Fes, Morocco

ISSN 2662-589X ISSN 2662-5903 (electronic)
Political Campaigning and Communication
ISBN 978-3-031-45142-3 ISBN 978-3-031-45143-0 (eBook)
https://doi.org/10.1007/978-3-031-45143-0

© The Editor(s) (if applicable) and The Author(s), under exclusive license to Springer
Nature Switzerland AG 2024

This work is subject to copyright. All rights are solely and exclusively licensed by the
Publisher, whether the whole or part of the material is concerned, specifically the rights
of translation, reprinting, reuse of illustrations, recitation, broadcasting, reproduction on
microfilms or in any other physical way, and transmission or information storage and
retrieval, electronic adaptation, computer software, or by similar or dissimilar methodology
now known or hereafter developed.
The use of general descriptive names, registered names, trademarks, service marks, etc.
in this publication does not imply, even in the absence of a specific statement, that such
names are exempt from the relevant protective laws and regulations and therefore free for
general use.
The publisher, the authors, and the editors are safe to assume that the advice and information in this book are believed to be true and accurate at the date of publication. Neither
the publisher nor the authors or the editors give a warranty, expressed or implied, with
respect to the material contained herein or for any errors or omissions that may have been
made. The publisher remains neutral with regard to jurisdictional claims in published maps
and institutional affiliations.

Cover illustration: Location Elements/Stockimo/Alamy Stock Photo

This Palgrave Macmillan imprint is published by the registered company Springer Nature
Switzerland AG
The registered company address is: Gewerbestrasse 11, 6330 Cham, Switzerland

Paper in this product is recyclable.

*To my beloved family which never stopped believing in me.
For my kids whose laughter is my favorite sound.*

For my friends who taught me the true meaning of friendship.

To you, dear reader, for making this journey worthwhile.

ACKNOWLEDGEMENTS

I would like to extend my thanks and gratitude to the people whose help was a milestone in the completion of this book. I recognize the invaluable assistance that you all provided during my research.

I wish to express my sincere appreciation to my colleagues Dr. Abdelhalim Larbi and Dr. Said Saddiki whose advice, guidance and encouragement proved monumental towards the success of this book.

I also wish to acknowledge my family's great support and love. They kept me going and this book would not have been possible without their prayers and encouragement.

CONTENTS

1 **Introduction**   1
Foreign Policy Analysis (FPA): Relating the Definitions
and Theoretical Approaches to the Units of Analysis   2
  Foreign Policy and Foreign Policy Making: Definitions
  and General Trends   2
  Foreign Policy Analysis (FPA): A Brief Overview
  of the Theoretical Approaches   4
  The Scope of the Book: Relating the Definitions
  and the Theoretical Approaches to the Units of Analysis   5
The Relationship Between Mass Media, Public Opinion
Interest Groups and Foreign Policy: Synthesizing
the Conceptual and Theoretical Debate   8
  Mass Media and Foreign Policy: A Glimpse of the Literature   8
  The Relation Between the Public Opinion and Foreign
  Policy Making: A Glance at the Scholarly Debate   13
  The Influential Role of Interest Groups on Policymaking:
  The Conceptual and Theoretical Explanation   17
  The Political Impact of Think Tanks: The Scholarly
  Debate, Methodological Constraints, and Multiple-stream
  Theory   21

2 **The Media and US Foreign Policy in the MENA Area:**
From the *War on Terror* to the *Arab Spring*   25

x CONTENTS

*The Presidential Discourse from 9/11 to the Arab Spring:
From a Rhetoric of Fear to a Rhetoric of Democracy* 26
  *George W. Bush and the Rhetoric of Fear in the Post-9/11
  Era: Setting the Agenda for the Media* 26
  Barack Obama: A Temporary Change from Bush's Rhetoric 47

**3 The US Public Opinion: A Marginal Impact on US
Foreign Policy** 67
  *Ronald Reagan and US Intervention in Lebanon
  (1982–1984): A Complete Disinterest in the American
  Public Opinion* 67
    *The Pre-1983 Bombings on US Marines: Reagan's
    Disinterest in the Public Disapproval of US Military
    Presence in Lebanon* 67
    *The Post-1983 Bombings on US Marines: A Continual
    Disinterest in Public Opinion* 68
  *George H. W. Bush and the Gulf War (1990–1991):
  A Halfhearted Appeal to the Public Opinion* 70
  Bill Clinton and Iraq: A Strong Public Opinion Support 73
  *George W Bush and the War on Terror: The Rise and the Fall
  of the Presidential Manipulation of US Public Opinion* 74
    *9/11 and Fear: An Insidious Presidential Manipulation
    of the Public Opinion* 74
    The War on Iraq: A Strong Support of US Public Opinion 75
    *The Post-War Era: The Fall of Bush Rhetoric and the Shift
    in the US Public Opinion* 76
  *Barack Obama and the Arab Uprisings: A Partial Appeal
  to Public Opinion* 77
    *The American Intervention in Libya: A Skeptical
    but Supportive Public Opinion* 77
    *Obama and the Syrian Crisis: An Unprecedented Public
    Opinion Impact on the President's War Plans* 79

4 Interest Groups: An Imperfect Impact 83
  Interest Groups: Definitions and Classification 83
    Interest Groups: A Broadly Defined Concept 83
    Interest Groups: A Variously Categorized Concept 84
    American Israel Public Affairs Committee (AIPAC) 87

AIPAC's Lobbying Strategies: A Multivariate Grass-root Approach to Shaping and Dominating the US Public Opinion 87
Gaining Access to Policymakers: Various Means, But One End 93
AIPAC and US Foreign Policy in the MENA Area: An Imperfect Influence 99

5 Think Tanks: A Circuitous Impact on US Foreign Policy 125
The Typologies of Think Tanks in the US 126
Universities Without Students/Academic Think Tanks 127
Contract Think Tanks 128
Advocacy Think Tanks 128
The Impact of US Think Tanks on US Foreign Policy in the MENA Region: Case Studies 130
William J. Clinton (1993–2001) and the Shift in US Foreign Policy: A Significant But Ambivalent Impact of Think Tanks 130
George W. Bush (2001–2009): A Circuitous Impact of Conservative Think Tanks 136
Barack Obama (2009–2017): A Unique Case in Many Ways 143

Summary and Conclusion 151

References 161

Index 171

LIST OF FIGURES

Fig. 2.1   Political-media effects on public opinion on the *War on Terror*: November 2001-January 2002 (*Source* Pew Research Center Surveys)   29

Fig. 2.2   Public attention to Iraq (December 2003–April 2008) (*Source* Pew Resource Center)   40

Fig. 2.3   The relationship between reporting on the absence of WMDs in Iraq and the Americans' opinion about the war (*Source* Pew Research Center Surveys [February 2004])   42

Fig. 2.4   The relationship between Abu Ghraib scandal and public opposition to war (*Source* Pew Research Center Surveys [April 2004])   43

Fig. 2.5   The relationship between attention to news on Iraq and mistreatment at Guantanamo to Americans' support to a withdrawal from Iraq (*Source* Pew Research Center Surveys [February, June and December 2004])   44

Fig. 2.6   Public opinion on Iran (February 2006–December 2012) (*Sources* CNN, NBC News/ Wall Street Journal, Gallup and CBS News surveys)   51

Fig. 2.7   The impact of the US media's coverage of Benghazi on Obama's credibility (*Source* Pew Research Center Survey [September and October, 2012])   60

xiii

CHAPTER 1

Introduction

This book examines how US media, public opinion, interest groups and think tanks respond to US Presidents' attempts to market their foreign policies in the MENA region. Additionally, we discuss whether these responses yield an impact on US foreign policy in this strategic area. In so doing, the book answers the following question: Who influences whom in US foreign policy decision making pertaining to the Middle East and North Africa?

As for media and interest groups, the scope of the analysis extends from the war on terror to the so-called Arab Spring, which coincided with the presidencies of George Bush and Barack Obama. The analysis of the influence of public opinion extends from Ronald Reagan to Barack Obama. The examination of the impactful role of think tanks will be carried out in the light of three presidencies; namely, Bill Clinton, George Bush, and Barack Obama. We examined relevant case studies including critical issues and events such as the Arab-Israeli conflict, the Iran nuclear deal, the *war on terror,* and the *Arab Spring.*

This introductory chapter proceeds as follows: It starts with briefly defining foreign policy and foreign policy making through presenting the general trends and the theoretical approaches in Foreign Policy Analysis (FPA). The chapter relates these definitions and theoretical approaches to the book's units of analysis, which constitute the focus of each chapter;

© The Author(s), under exclusive license to Springer Nature Switzerland AG 2024
F. Touzani, *Marketing US Foreign Policy in the MENA Region,* Political Campaigning and Communication,
https://doi.org/10.1007/978-3-031-45143-0_1

1

namely, media, public opinion, think tanks, and interest groups. This introduction finishes with presenting a brief synthesis of the conceptual and theoretical debate pertaining to the relationship between foreign policy making and the media, public opinion interest groups, and think tanks. In so doing, we will discuss the role of these non-state actors in initiating or influencing foreign policy making.

FOREIGN POLICY ANALYSIS (FPA): RELATING THE DEFINITIONS AND THEORETICAL APPROACHES TO THE UNITS OF ANALYSIS

Foreign Policy and Foreign Policy Making: Definitions and General Trends

As a major sub-field of International Relations, foreign policy seems to be an elusive concept as there is a lack of consensual definition among IR scholars. However, most definitions tend to focus on the actions of the state as the central agent in foreign policy.

Christopher Hill defined foreign policy as "the sum of official external relations conducted by an independent actor (usually a state) in international relations".[1] A similar and more recent definition was provided by Morin and Paquin who considered foreign policy as "a set of actions or rules governing the actions of an independent political authority deployed in the international environment".[2] A more detailed definition of foreign policy came from Carlsnaes, Risse, and Simmons who elaborated more on what constitutes a "state", the state's actions as well as the targets of foreign policy:

> Those actions which, expressed in the form of explicitly stated goals, commitments and/or directives, and pursued by governmental representatives acting on behalf of their sovereign communities, are directed

---

[1] Christopher Hill, *The Changing Politics of Foreign Policy* (Palgrave, 2003), p. 3.

[2] Jean-Frédéric Morin and Jonathan Paquin, *Foreign Policy Analysis: A Toolbox* (Springer, 2018), p. 3.

towards objectives, conditions and actors- both governmental and non-governmental- which they want to affect and which lie beyond their territorial legitimacy.[3]

These definitions imply an important argument about the concept of foreign policy making. Foreign policy making is a process that involves internal actors whose foreign policy decisions are prompted by external factors. The internal actors are, first and foremost, the states and their agents such as kings or presidents and parliaments or congresses. The foreign policy decisions of these state agents are mainly prompted by actions from external entities. Therefore, foreign policy generally aims at pursuing the state's national interests through affecting these external entities.

However, the fact that state actors act on behalf of their constituencies necessitates taking domestic factors into consideration while making foreign policy decisions. This requires state actors to make rational decisions through a careful examination of different alternatives in order to find compromises between domestic constraints and foreign goals. In so saying, foreign policy making has become a "democratized" process which involves state and non-state actors. Non-state actors represent the domestic constraints. Thus, they try to influence foreign policy decisions through different means. In fact, some contemporary definitions of foreign policy recognize the role of non-state actors in influencing foreign policies such as the definition suggested by Smith, Hadfield, and Dunne:

> Foreign policy, although traditionally linked to the behavior of states, can apply equally to explaining the behavior of a range of other actors. Thus, it is perfectly possible to speak of international organizations, transnational companies, regional governments, transnational terrorist groups and a variety of other non-state-based actors as having and deploying foreign policies.[4]

In democratic societies such as the US, the state derives its legitimacy from its interaction with citizens as well as the institutions that represent

---

[3] Walter Carlsnaes, Thomas Risse, and Beth A. Simmons, *Handbook of International Relations* (Sage Publications, 2012), p. 335.

[4] Steve Smith, Amelia Hadfield, and Tim Dunne, *Foreign Policy: Theories, Actors, Cases* (Oxford University Press, 2016), p. 2.

them and articulate their interests. These societal institutions are the non-state actors which may play a constraining role on the state's function to make foreign policies as Waltz put it: "States are not and never have been the only international actors ...[and] ... importance of nonstate actors and the extent of transnational activities are obvious".[5]

In the US and in addition to the public opinion, non-state actors include political parties, media, think tanks, and various types of interest groups. From these definitions that provide a broad idea of what is foreign policy and who makes it, we can say that while state actors remain at the heart of foreign policy making, non-state actors may play a crucial constraining role on the state actors' constitutional function to make foreign policy.

Foreign Policy Analysis (FPA): A Brief Overview of the Theoretical Approaches

Foreign policy is analyzed in the light of different theoretical approaches. While some of these approaches are exclusively conceptualized to analyze foreign policy, others are borrowed from the mother discipline of International Relations (IR). We can differentiate between three major groups of theoretical approaches that aim at making sense of foreign policy; namely, traditional, behavioral, and contemporary approaches.

Traditional Approaches

The traditional approaches of foreign policy analysis are borrowed from the broader discipline of International Relations. Traditional theories of IR argue that the nature of the international system has a great impact on foreign policy decisions. In so saying, they focus on the state's pursuit of self-interest as the major factor that guides foreign policy making. This is often referred to as the rational-choice theory.[6] The most important traditional approaches are idealism and realism.

---

[5] Kenneth Waltz, *Theory of International Politics* (Reading, MA: Addison-Wesley Publication, 1979), pp. 93–94.

[6] Chris Alden and Amnon Aran, *Foreign Policy Analysis: New Approaches* (Routledge, 2017), p. 6.

Behavioral Approaches

The main focus of behavioral approaches is to understand and explain how foreign policy decisions are made. Behavioralists criticize traditional approaches for basing their understating of human nature on presupposed assumptions. According to behavioral approaches, foreign policy decisions should be explained based on observable data including the actions, circumstances, and environment of individuals as well as the processes and motives leading to these decisions.[7] Therefore, these approaches' major unit of analysis is the individual rather than the state.

Behavioralists also criticize the traditional approaches' absolute understanding of rationality. They argue that rationality is restrained by other factors that should be taken into consideration while analyzing foreign policy.[8] There exist different behavioral approaches in FPA. These include decision-making approach, comparative foreign policy approach, case study approach, event-data approach, prospect theory approach, and role theory approach.

Contemporary Approaches

Contemporary theories of IR were the outcome of many criticisms of traditional theories. Contemporary theories share one assumption about international relations. That is, they are socially constructed. The major contemporary approaches of FPA are constructivism and neo-classical realism.

The Scope of the Book: Relating the Definitions and the Theoretical Approaches to the Units of Analysis

A close examination of the previously discussed definitions and theoretical approaches of Foreign Policy Analysis reveals that foreign policy decisions are made by state actors and might be influenced by domestic non-state actors as well as external factors. To put it differently, there are three units of analysis in foreign policy making, which are also factors that contribute

---

[7] Charles W. Kegley, *World Politics: Trend and Transformation* (Wadsworth Publishing 12th Edition, 2008), p. 48.

[8] Richard Ned Lebow and Nathan Funk (Eds.), Richard Ned Lebow: A Pioneer in International Relations Theory, History, *Political Philosophy and Psychology* (Springer, 2017), p. 38.

6   F. TOUZANI

to making and influencing foreign policy decisions. These include individual, internal, and external factors. This book will examine some of these factors in the context of US foreign policy in the Middle East and North Africa.

Individual Factors: The Role of the American President as the Major Foreign Policy Maker
The majority of foreign policy analysts focus on states' leaders as the major units of analyses in foreign policy making. The Rational Actor Model in FPA argues that leaders are rational actors, which means that they try to attain their states' national interests through a cost-benefit analysis of different policy options in order to single out the one that would maximize their states' power and ensure their survival in the international system.[9] To do so, leaders have to be aware of the different dimensions of the problem at stake including other parties' positions, the policy options at hand as well as potential constraints.

On the other hand, the cognitive school of thought claims that leaders are not as rational as they are thought to be because their rational behavior might be influenced by some psychological and social factors such as their personal experiences, attitudes, beliefs, and ideologies as well as the members of their governments. All of these might affect their perceptions of the external environment.[10]

Internal factors: State and Non-state Actors in US Foreign Policy

According to the liberal International Relations theory, the most influential internal factors that are believed to shape foreign policy making include states' political systems, political parties, media, public opinion, epistemic communities, and interest groups.[11] These internal factors can be classified in two categories: State and non-state actors.

---

[9] Laura Neack, *The New Foreign Policy* (Lanham, MD: Rowman & Littlefield Publishers, 2008), pp. 31–39.

[10] Ibid., 47–64.

[11] Marijke Breuning, *Foreign Policy Analysis: A Comparative Introduction* (Springer, 2007), pp. 115–140.

1 INTRODUCTION 7

Congress: The Major State Co-maker of US Foreign Policy
The state actors relate to the nature of the states' political system and their political institutional structure. For example, in a democratic political system like the US, the power of foreign policy making is divided between the President and Congress. Each checks and balances the foreign policy decisions of the other.[12]

Non-state Internal Actors in US Foreign Policy: A Constraining Role?
The importance of non-state domestic actors in shaping foreign policy making also relates to the nature of the states' political system and the structure of their political institutions. In an open liberal democratic system like the US, the role of non-state actors in influencing foreign policy making is more likely to be influential unlike authoritarian regimes whose foreign policy decisions are almost exclusively taken by leaders.[13]

To illustrate, the media and the public opinion are considered to be impactful internal non-state actors in foreign policy making, especially in open liberal societies which value the freedom of the press and the freedom of expression in general. However, the central question in this regard is: Who uses whom? In other words, do leaders use media to shape public opinion in favor of their foreign policy decisions or do media and public opinion manage to have effective effects on decision makers' foreign policy? These are some of the questions we will answer in this book in the context of US foreign policy in the MENA region.

Other internal factors include epistemic communities or what some prefer to call think tanks. Think tanks are independent, non-profit organizations that aim at affecting policies through producing and spreading scholarly research in conferences, seminars, books, papers, reports, and journals.[14] Unlike the role of think tanks in Europe, their role in the US is considered important due to several factors. The most significant factor is party discipline. While the executive and legislative representatives of political parties in Europe tend to respect the policy advice provided

---

[12] Scott Burchill, Liberalism Scott Burchill, et al. (Eds.), *Theories of International Relations*, Fourth Edition (New York: Palgrave Macmillan, 2009), pp. 60–73.

[13] Breuning, *Foreign Policy Analysis: A Comparative Introduction* (2007), pp. 120–125.

[14] Many prominent scholars have given different definitions to the term "think tank". These include Abelson (2009), McGann & Weaver (2000) and Stone and Denham (2004), to name a few.

8   F. TOUZANI

by their political parties, American presidents and members of Congress are not obliged to conform to their parties' policy commands.[15] Consequently, they are more likely to seek the expertise of think tanks to help them make domestic and foreign policies.

Last but not least, it is difficult to talk about internal factors that shape foreign policy without mentioning the role of interest or lobby groups and civil society organizations, especially in liberal democracies like the US. These groups try to influence decision makers through direct lobbying mechanisms or through grass-root activities that aim at mobilizing US public opinion to put pressure on decision makers.[16] Interest groups differ in their aims as well as their abilities to have access to decision makers due to their financial resources and organizational capabilities. The American Israel Public Affairs Committee (AIPAC) is claimed to be the most influential interest group when discussing US foreign policy in the MENA area.[17]

THE RELATIONSHIP BETWEEN MASS MEDIA, PUBLIC OPINION INTEREST GROUPS AND FOREIGN POLICY: SYNTHESIZING THE CONCEPTUAL AND THEORETICAL DEBATE

Mass Media and Foreign Policy: A Glimpse of the Literature

The relationship between media and foreign policy decision making has been widely debated among scholars of political sciences and media studies. These debates examine relevant questions pertaining to the role of media in setting the foreign policy agenda and their impact on the process of formulating foreign policies. Taking into consideration that there are no well-established theories explaining a clear causal influence of media on formulating policies in general, there are two major scholarly directions that guide the literature on the relationship between media and foreign policies.

---

[15] Diane Stone, Introduction. Think Tanks, Policy Advice and Governance. In Diane Stone and Andrew Denham (Eds.): *Think Tanks Traditions, Policy Research, and Politics of Ideas* (Manchester University Press, 2004), pp. 1–16 (pp. 1–2).

[16] Ibid., 31.

[17] Jefferey H. Birnbaum, "Washington's Poser 25," Fortune, December 8, 1997.

The first scholarly direction is illustrated by the *CNN Effect* theory. Feist stated: "CNN effect is a theory that compelling television images, such as images of a humanitarian crisis, cause U.S. policymakers to intervene in a situation when such an intervention might otherwise not be in the U.S. national interest".[18] Livingston and Eachus considered the theory "as elite decision makers' loss of policy control to news media".[19] Schorr described the theory as "the way breaking news affects foreign policy decisions".[20] These definitions support the argument that the media, and television in particular, exert a powerful influence on policymaking. However, some scholars minimize these influential powers claiming that the *CNN Effect* is limited to humanitarian cases because a continuous display of images of mass starvation on the news prompts policymakers to react and intervene in such cases.[21] In fact, the CNN Effect theory originated in few humanitarian cases. One of these cases was the US military intervention in Somalia in 1992 through *Operation Restore Hope* which aimed at feeding people in Somalia and preventing a humanitarian disaster, especially after the fall of the local government and the spread of anarchy. Proponents of the CNN Effect theory argue that the continuous CNN coverage of the humanitarian crisis prompted the US to intervene in the country.

On the other hand, critics of the CNN Effect show that the scholarly studies of the theory often lead to contradictory findings. As a result, they question the validity of the causative relationship between the media and foreign policy decision making.[22] For example, Gowing conducted a series of interviews with US government officials during the

---

[18] Samuel Feist, "Facing Down the Global Village: The Media Impact," in Kugier and E. Frost (Eds.): *The Global Century* (Washington, DC: National Defense University Press, 2001), pp. 709–725.

[19] Steven Livingston and Todd Eachus, "Humanitarian Crises and U.S. Foreign Policy: Somalia and the CNN Effect Reconsidered," Political Communication 12 (1995): 413.

[20] Daniel Schorr, "CNN Effect: Edge-of-Seat Diplomacy," Christian Science Monitor, November 27, 1998: 11.

[21] These include but not limited to Natsios' "Illusions of Influence: The CNN Effect in Complex Emergencies"; Gowing's "Real- Time Television Coverage" and Mermin's "Television News and American Intervention in Somalia. Jonathan Mermin, "Television News and American Intervention in Somalia: The Myth of a Media-Driven Foreign Policy" (1997).

[22] Eytan Gilboa, "The CNN Effect: The Search for a Communication Theory of International Relations," Political Communication 22 (2005): 36.

1990s and concluded that the impact of media on *strategic* US foreign policy decisions, which involve intervening during a humanitarian crisis, was relatively uncommon.[23] According to Gowing, the minor, or as he called *cosmetic* and *tactical*, policy responses to media pressure aimed at deviating the attention of the media from more significant interventions.[24] Livingston and Eachus carried out another study which analyzed the Operation Restore Hope in Somalia and concluded that the policymakers influenced the media more than the other way around.[25] Bennett explained that the media coverage of this case was simply indexed to the policy convictions of the political elites who were already convinced of the necessity to intervene in Somalia.[26]

Apart from these two opposite directions about the relationship between media and foreign policy decision making, a significant part of the literature concludes that the potential impact of media on policymaking depends on several factors. These include but are not limited to the type of problem under consideration and the political circumstances in action. To put it differently, the media are less likely to influence policymaking in situations of high risk, which might result in human casualties. In such situations, policymakers are prompted by other concerns that do not include media pressure. This is often referred to as the "body-bag Effect". For instance, the case of the US intervention in Northern Iraq in 1991 to protect Kurdish refugees was mainly motivated by geo-strategic factors including maintaining Turkey's stability which was endangered by the one million Kurdish refugees who were moving toward the southern part of Turkey.[27] In so saying, the coverage of the Kurdish refugee crisis did not have a strong influence on the US decision to intervene.[28] In contrast, when the political conditions involve no or little risk, the media

---

[23] Nik Gowing, "Real-Time Television Coverage of Armed Conflicts and Diplomatic Crises: Does It Pressure or Distort Foreign Policy Decisions?" John F. Kennedy School of Government, Harvard University (1994).

[24] Ibid.

[25] Livingston and Eachus, "Humanitarian Crises and U.S. Foreign Policy," 424.

[26] Lance W. Bennett, "Toward a Theory of Press-State Relations in the United States," *Journal of Communication* 40 (2) (1990): 114.

[27] Piers Robinson, *The CNN Effect: The Myth of News, Foreign Policy and Intervention* (New York and London: Routledge, 2002), p. 67.

[28] Piers Robinson, "The Policy-Media Interaction Model: Measuring Media Power During Humanitarian Crisis," *Journal of Peace Research* 37 (5) (2000): 620.

may have more influence on foreign policymaking.[29] The US military intervention in Zaire in 1994 is a case in point. The intervention was non-coercive and its major aim was to offer food and water to people of Zaire. In such a case, the intervention was mostly prompted by pressure from the media.

Most of the research on the CNN effect were carried out in the 1990s and they were mainly limited to the impact of news networks on US foreign policymaking with a focus on US interventions for humanitarian purposes. However, the *war on terror* and the *Arab Spring* coincided with the advance of the internet and the global media, especially in the MENA area. Additionally, US foreign policy decisions to intervene in the MENA area during the *war on terror* and the *Arab Spring* were not all prompted by humanitarian factors.

The twenty-first century witnessed the rise of the internet and portable technologies such as cell phones. These technologies have allowed users to take videos and pictures of important events and spread them all over the world in few seconds. Such events are also reported and broadcasted by print and global media networks such as the *CNN* and *Al Jazeera*. This has established an unprecedented level of transparency in media coverage of critical events and allowed journalists to rely less on official sources, which makes the indexing theory less prevalent. Such a quick and extensive spread of information may have more influence on decision makers because these latter have had less control on the flow of information in the internet epoch. *Wikileaks* and the secret information they uncovered about the *war on terror* as well as the role of social media in the Arab uprisings against the Arab authoritarian regimes are cases in point. However, the abundant flow of information is to be received with a great caution because a significant number of this information can be fake and fraudulent.

Mass Media and Foreign Policy: The Theoretical Frameworks
The theories that deal with the relationship between media and policy makers suggest two possible directions of influence. The first considers the media as an *input* variable as they influence the process of foreign

---

[29] Samuel Livingston, "Clarifying the CNN Effect: An examination of Media Effects According to Type of Military Intervention," Research Paper R-18, June (Cambridge, MA: The Joan Shorenstein Barone Center on the Press, Politics and Public Policy at Harvard University, 1997).

12   F. TOUZANI

policy decision making. The second direction considers the media as an *output* variable because they are influenced by the political elites through the public relations (PR) campaigns they establish.

Media as a Foreign Policy Influencer
The media as a foreign policy influencer is explained by two theories: Framing and agenda setting. The agenda-setting theory was first developed by Max McCombs. He argues that media play an important role in influencing the choice of important issues in the public agenda through increasing the salience of particular topics as they are frequently and dominantly covered.[30] Bernard Cohen introduces the concept of agenda setting to foreign policy making. He explained its function stating: "while [the press] may not be successful much of the time in telling people what to think, but it is stunningly successful in telling its readers what to think about. The world will look different to different people".[31]

The second theory is *framing*. It suggests that the way a particular issue is presented to the public, which is referred to as the *frame*, shapes the public opinion and the political elites through promoting specific interpretations using techniques such as stories, stereotypes, metaphors, and symbols.[32] We can say that while the agenda-setting theory focuses on *what* is talked about, the framing theory concentrates on *how* the issue talked about is understood and viewed.

Media as a Transmitter of Foreign Policy Convictions
This direction of influence is explained by the media management (MM) or the *spin* concept. It is a type of propaganda which aims at using manipulative techniques in PR campaigns to convince the media and the public opinion of the validity of a particular agenda.[33] In so doing,

---

[30] Maxwell McCombs and Amy Reynolds, "News Influence on our Pictures of the World," *Media Effects* (2002): 11–28.

[31] Bernard Cohen, *The Press and Foreign Policy* (Princeton University Press, 1963), 12–13.

[32] Shanto Iyengar and Adam Simon, "News Coverage of the Gulf Crisis and Public Opinion," In W. L. Bennett and D. L. Paletz (Eds.): *Taken by Storm: The Media, Public Opinion, and US Foreign Policy in the Gulf War* (Chicago: Chicago University Press, 1994), 171.

[33] See Pfetsch's. "Government News Management" for an overview oh how government can use the media to influence the public opinion.

policy makers rely on "spin doctors", or PR specialists and professionals in marketing, to serve this purpose using various methods. These include but are not limited to leaking information, briefings, press conferences, interviews, and media events.[34] The MM techniques are more likely to be used during conflicts and wars when policymakers precede or follow their foreign policy decisions with PR strategies. These include ignoring the media through an abstention from communicating messages to them, crafting a "spin", or making public announcements with no political action.[35]

The media tend to be more supportive of the decision makers' agenda when decision makers achieve a high level of public consensus. In this case, the "spin doctors" work on maintaining and strengthening this support. However, when decision makers fail to achieve such a public consensus, the media become more critical and the "spin doctors" renew their PR strategies to alter the media's attitude.[36]

The Relation Between the Public Opinion and Foreign Policy Making: A Glance at the Scholarly Debate

The role of American public opinion in shaping US foreign policy has been a topic of heated debates among academicians and policymakers. These debates were often translated into research questions that examine the relationship between public opinion and foreign policy making in the light of specific international contexts that often deal with US military interventions abroad. Questions such as: How do Americans develop their foreign policy opinion and what factors influence it? Is the American public opinion rational and consistent? Does the American public opinion play an impactful role in shaping US foreign policy?

The critical international issues, which often deal with wars or the use of force, prompt polling organizations, TV networks, or prominent newspapers to conduct surveys to find the attitudes and aptitudes of Americans

---

[34] See Cohen's *Media Diplomacy: The Foreign Office in the Mass Communications Age*, which examines how information leaking is used as one of the methods for media management.

[35] Chanan Naveh, "The Role of Media in Foreign Policy Decision Making: A Theoretical Framework," Conflict and Communication, 1 (2) (2002): 9.

[36] Gadi Wolfsfeld, *Media and Political Conflict: News From the Middle East* (Cambridge University Press, 1997), p. 25.

about these issues as well as to evaluate the American public opinion's level of support or opposition to foreign policy decisions taken by the executive or the legislative powers.

The scholarly debate on the relationship between public opinion and foreign policy making takes the results of opinion polls to a further step in order to examine to what extent the public opinion shapes US foreign policy. There are two divergent scholarly views which explain this relationship.

The first view argues that the public opinion's role in shaping American foreign policy remains very limited due to several factors. The most important factors are the general lack of interest in issues of foreign policy among Americans as well as the lack of transparent information about such issues. Consequently, the American public is more likely to adopt and follow the policies of state actors in foreign policy, especially the President.

The second view claims that the public opinion has become more consistent. Despite the fact that the public might not be well-informed about specific foreign policy issues or have vested interests in such issues, it does play a crucial role in shaping some foreign policy decisions. As a result, they are more likely to control and constrain the decisions of the major state actors in foreign policy, especially the President.

The Role of Public Opinion in Foreign Policy: The Theoretical Approaches

It is important to point out that there are many theoretical approaches which provide empirical or normative explanations to international relations or foreign policy decisions such as postmodernism and dependency theories. However, the realist and liberal theoretical approaches seem to be dominant among IR scholars and the makers of foreign policy. While the realist approach represents the classical understanding of international relations as it dates back to Thucydides, the liberal approach remains relatively modern as it emerged in the seventeenth century and coincided with the establishment of the modern state system.

The Liberal Approach and the Central Role of Public Opinion in Foreign Policy Making

According to the liberal approach, the public opinion lies at the heart of the foreign policy making process and it is considered a prerequisite for its effectiveness and legitimacy.[37] Jeremy Bentham, one of the most prominent liberal theorists, considered public opinion the "sole remedy" for possible shortcomings of government policy making.[38]

Generally speaking, the proponents of the liberal approach argue that the executive power takes the public opinion into consideration owing to several assumptions. To begin with, liberal theorists emphasize the importance of public opinion in legitimizing the executive power.[39] Additionally, the liberalists claim that rational leaders support their people's preferences and respect their will because they are behind their election.[40] Consequently, if leaders take decisions against the public's will, their reputation will be tarnished and they might not be re-elected.[41]

In a more specific context, Immanuel Kant expressed a similar argument with a focus on war as a critical example of foreign policy decisions. He argues that the public is more likely to play a key role in restricting the choice of war that some leaders may lean to in a Republican system unlike monarchy in which monarchs may be involved in a war whose motives are irrelevant to the citizens' interests.[42]

The Realist Approach and the Marginalized Role of Public Opinion in Foreign Policy Making

Generally speaking, the realist approach minimizes the impact of public opinion on foreign policy making due to several factors. The proponents of this theoretical framework argue that the public opinion is more likely to be characterized by irrationality, passion, lack of information, and

---

[37] Liberal scholars include but not limited to Holsti (1996), Shamir (2005) and Steven and Patrick (2009).

[38] Jeremy Bentham, *Works of Jeremy Bentham* (New York: Russell and Russell, 1962), vol. 8, p. 561.

[39] Yaacov Shamir, "Introduction: What Is Public Opinion and Why Is It Important to Conflict Resolution?" *Palestine-Israel Journal of Politics, Economics and Culture* 11 (4): 2005, https://pij.org/articles/304/introduction-what-is-public-opinion-and-why-is-it-important-to-conflict-resolution. Accessed January 9, 2020.

[40] Eugene R. Wittkopf and Christopher M. Jones, *American Foreign Policy: Pattern and Process* (New York: St Martin's Press, 2012), p. 265.

[41] Steve Chan and William Safran, "Public Opinion as a Constraint Against War: Democracies' Responses to Operation Iraqi Freedom," *Foreign Policy Analysis*, 2006, p. 167.

[42] Emmanuel Kant, *Perpetual Peace, and Other Essays on Politics, History, and Morals* (Indianapolis: Hackett, 1983) 113, introduced and translated by Ted Humphrey.

16 F. TOUZANI

volatility in addition to the possibility of being manipulated by the media or politicians.[43]

The first US realists were some of the founding fathers who were also the drafters of US Constitution. To illustrate, the *Federalist Papers* claimed that the Senate, whose members were appointed until 1918, is more likely to be effective in foreign policy making than the elected House of Representatives.[44]

Tocqueville expressed a similar argument which considered aristocracy as a "firm and enlightened body" unlike democracy whose public might be affected by ignorance and passion which constitute stumbling blocks to efficient foreign policy decisions.[45] As a matter of fact, ignorance and passion remain the major characteristics that realists use to question the effectiveness of public opinion in foreign policy making. In so saying, decision makers are more likely to neglect the ignorant and passionate public opinion when dealing with foreign policy issues because their passion and subjectivity are very unlikely to serve "national interests", which include maximizing the state's power in order to survive in an unstable world.[46]

Bachner and Ginsburg used numerous statistical data to prove that American government bureaucrats' policy preferences are different from those of most Americans. Additionally, they have different policy priorities and try to persuade the public of their policy convictions.[47]

The realists' view of the role of public opinion in policy making remains stronger in domestic affairs than in foreign ones. They claim that the public can be effective in shaping domestic policies because the issues under discussion are directly related to their everyday activities. Therefore, they tend to be enthusiastic and well-informed about such issues unlike

---

[43] Realists scholars include but not limited to Lippmann (1955), Knecht and Weatherford (2006), Robinson (2008). Jentleson (2013) and McCormick (2013).

[44] Alexander Hamilton, John Jay and James Madison, *The Federalist* (New York: Modern Library, 1037), p. 1788.

[45] Alexis de Tocqueville, *Democracy in America* (New York: Vintage, 1958), 1: 243–245.

[46] The most important contemporary neorealist scholar who supports this argument are John Mearsheimer in his article "American Public Opinion and the Special Relationship with Israel".

[47] Jennifer Bachner and Benjamin Ginsberg, *America's State Governments: A Critical Look at Disconnected Democracies* (Routledge, 2020).

foreign ones about which the public tend to be less informed and less motivated because they think that foreign issues are not directly related to their daily lives.[48]

The lack of information about foreign affairs among the public is taken advantage of by policymakers who can persuade it to follow their opinion and accept their foreign policy decisions through framing the problem in a specific manner.[49] The spread of information technologies may weaken the realists' claim that public opinion is less informed about foreign policy issues. However, the way such issues are framed by politicians and media may influence the public opinion.

The Influential Role of Interest Groups on Policymaking: The Conceptual and Theoretical Explanation

To begin with, it is important to point out that the concept of influence involves all stages of policy making process from setting the agenda to the effective execution of policies.[50] In so saying, the political influence of interest groups remains a multidimensional process that constitutes of different phases.

A Conceptual Framework for the Political Influence of Interest Groups: A Multi-stage Process

The first stage necessitates choosing effective lobbying strategies and tactics. It requires interest groups to make effective use of some strategies and tactics in order to exert political influence on policymakers.[51] These lobbying mechanisms can take direct and indirect forms. To illustrate, an interest group may opt for a grass-root campaign that involves

---

[48] Benjamin I. Page and Robert Y. Shapiro, *The Rational Public: Fifty Years of Trends in Americans' Policy Preferences* (Chicago: University of Chicago Press, 1992); Alan D. Monroe, Public Opinion and Public Policy, 1980–1993, Public Opinion Quarterly 62 (1) (May) (1998): 6–28. https://doi.org/10.1086/297828.

[49] George W. Bush was able to persuade Americans of the necessity to attack Iraq because Saddam Hussein possessed WMDs and helped terrorists taking advantage of the atmosphere of fear that prevailed after 9/11.

[50] Patrick Bernhagen, "Who Gets What in British Politics—And How? An Analysis of Media Reports on Lobbying around Government Policies, 2001–7, *Political Studies* (2011): 1–21.

[51] Raj Chari, John Hogan, Gary Murphy and Michele Crepaz, *Regulating Lobbying: A Global Comparison* (Manchester University Press, 2019).

18   F. TOUZANI

inciting the public opinion to put the legislators or the executives under pressure through calling them, writing to them, and organizing protests before voting on a law or taking a decision on an important issue.[52]

Another direct lobbying technique includes Political Action Committees (PACs) whose number and importance has increasingly grown in American politics. The PACs' main function is to raise funds and use them to finance the campaigns of political candidates who are more likely to serve their interests when they get into power. A PAC can be part of an interest group as it can also be independent.[53] A further lobbying mechanism is resorting to courts, especially when members of Congress or the President choose to be indifferent to their concerns or not find interests in them.[54]

The second stage focuses on gaining access to policymakers. The use of good lobbying strategies and techniques allows interest groups to gain access to decision makers.[55] The level of access differs from one interest group to another due to several factors.[56] The most important factors are the size and financial resources. Interest groups which have larger and dedicated members as well as access to more financial resources are

---

[52] Few recent studies found that lobbying through calling or sending messages to legislators is not as effective as most theories of grassroots lobbying claim. See, for example, John Cluverius, "How the Flattened Costs of Grassroots Lobbying Affect Legislator Responsiveness", *Political Research Quarterly* (2017) https://doi.org/10.1177%2F1 065912916688110.

[53] Alexander Fouirnaies and Andrew Hall provide evidence of how interest groups seek to influence policies through their campaign contributions and other means. See their article "How Do Interest Groups Seek Access to Committees?" American Journal of Political Science (2017), https://doi.org/10.1111/ajps.12323. Accessed March 20, 2020.

[54] Stephen Wasby provides a good explanation of the factors that influence litigations brought by interest groups. See "Interest groups and litigation", *Policy Studies Journal* (2005): 657–670. https://doi.org/10.1111/j.1541-0072.1983.tb0 0569.x. Accessed March 20, 2020.

[55] Jan Beyers and Caelesta Braun, "Ties That Count: Explaining Interest Group Access to Policymakers," *Journal of Public Policy* 34 (1) (2014): 93–121.

[56] Different scholars have discussed the importance of having access to policymakers as a prerequisite to influence policies. These include Pieter Bouwen, "Corporate Lobbying: Towards a Theory of Access," Journal of European Public Policy (2002): 365–390 and Jan Beyers, "Gaining and Seeking Access: The European Adaptation of Domestic Interest Associations," European Journal of Political Research (2002): 585–612.

generally more likely to be effective and successful in impacting policies.[57] To put it differently, larger interest groups with dedicated members can be very effective in organizing influential grass-root campaigns that aim at garnering public opinion support for a specific issue. Furthermore, interest groups with larger financial resources can be politically influential through their contributions to Political Action Committees.

Other factors include leadership and internal cohesion.[58] Whether they are professional lobbyists or charismatic leaders, a prominent leadership is very crucial for gaining a greater access to policymakers. Additionally, internal cohesion is fundamental to attaining greater access to policymakers. This cohesion is often found in interest groups whose members share the same or similar ethnic, ideological, or foreign policy goals.

The third stage aims at influencing the policy making. Choosing effective lobbying strategies and tactics as well as gaining access to policymakers are very likely to result in influencing policy decisions from setting the agenda to shaping policies. However, the levels of influence generally depend on how interest groups use effective lobbying techniques as well as on the degree of access to policymakers in addition to the political systems in which they function, which we discuss in the following paragraphs.

The Theoretical Explanation to the Interest Groups: Pluralism vs. Neo-corporatism
The major theoretical perspectives that explain the impact of interest groups on policymaking are pluralism and neo-corporatism.

The pluralist theory considers politics and policymaking as a marketplace where various different ideas and perspectives, generated by individuals, political parties and interest groups, compete to get their voices

---

[57] Few studies provide some empirical findings about the lack of importance of interest groups financial resources in influencing policy making. See, for example, Beth Leech, Frank Baumgartner, Jefferey Berry, Marie Hojnacki, and David Kimball, "Does Money Buy Power? Interest Group Resources and Policy Outcomes", Paper Presented at the Annual Meeting of the Midwest Political Science Association, Chicago, April 12–15, 2007, https://fbaum.unc.edu/papers/MPSA_2007_Does_Money_Buy_Power.pdf. Accessed March 19, 2020.

[58] Hahrie Han, Kenneth T. Andrews, Marshall Ganz, Matthew Baggetta, and Chaeyoon Lim nicely described the relationship between the leadership of interest groups and their political influence in their article "The Relationship of Leadership Quality to the Political Presence of Civic Associations," *Perspectives on Politics* 9 (1) (2011): 45–59.

20   F. TOUZANI

heard by policymakers.[59] In so saying, the pluralist theory in political science provides a realistic account of the relationship that exists between interest groups and policymakers, especially in liberal democracies such as the US.

According to the pluralist view, the fact that there is competition in a free political market of interests prevents a potential monopoly of interests by a specific group, which results in having a balanced access to policymakers and a regulated influence on policymaking. However, there are many factors that may disrupt this presumed balance resulting in making some interest groups more powerful than others in terms of gaining access to policymakers and influencing policy making.

The first factors relate to the possession of financial and human resources which might make well-financed and well-organized interest groups more likely to gain noticeable access to policymakers and exert effective influence on policymaking than those less organized and less financed interest groups.

Another factor relates to the role of government in resolving conflicts, which is less likely to be neutral. The government is more likely to adopt specific groups' interests because they relate to the state's interests such as the oil and gas firms in relation to US foreign policy in the MENA area. In fact, these factors are taken into consideration by the elitist theory which is considered a modified version of the pluralist theory.[60]

The other theoretical perspective is corporatism and its modified version, the neo-corporatist theory. This approach considers the policymaking process as the product of institutional cooperation between policymakers and some interest groups, especially those who have economic interests.[61]

The corporatist political system has many characteristics some of which relate to the influence of interest groups, especially the economic and

---

[59] The most prominent pluralist theoretical references include Robert Dahl's *Who Governs?* and David Truman's *The Governmental Process: Political Interests and Public Opinion.*

[60] The most prominent *elitist* scholar is Theodore J. Lowi who published many books on this theory the most important of which is The End of Liberalism: The Second Republic of the United States.

[61] PerOla Öberg, Torsten Svensson, Peter Munk Christiansen, Asbjø Sonne Nørgaard, Hillary Rommetvedt and Gunnar Thesen, "Disrupted Exchange and Declining Corporatism: Government Authority and Interest Group Capability in Scandinavia," *Government and Opposition* 46 (3) (2001): 365–391.

business ones. First, business interest groups are more likely to be a small but strong community that clusters in one influential federation.[62] Second, the state tends to be more involved in the economy with a focus on spending less on defense and more on social welfare programs. In so saying, it is difficult to think of the US as a corporatist country because the federal state does not engage in institutional cooperation with business interest groups and the US is generally known for its high expenditures on defense.

The Political Impact of Think Tanks: The Scholarly Debate, Methodological Constraints, and Multiple-stream Theory

Scholarly Debates and Methodological Constraints

The impact of US think tanks on US foreign policy has been widely debated among political scientists. David Ricci argues that US think tanks play a crucial role in shaping US foreign policy. However, he thinks that political scientists have not recognized their new, important, and institutional impact on American foreign policy decision making.[63]

Abelson argues that because of methodological constraints, it is very difficult to assess the impact of think tanks on foreign policy decision making. This is especially true when the discussion revolves around establishing a causal relationship between the decisions taken by policy makers and the policy recommendations made by different think tanks.[64] Similarly, Stone describes the impact of think tanks on policymaking as diffuse, variable, and hard to measure.[65]

Some scholars explain the impact of think tanks on US foreign policy by the fracturing of the policy making process, which results from the

[62] Peter Munk Christiansen, Asbjørn Sonne Nørgaard, Hilmar Rommetvedt, Torsten Svensson, Gunnar Thesen, and PerOla Öberg, "Varieties of Democracy: Interest Groups and Corporatist Committees in Scandinavian Policy Making," *Voluntas: International Journal of Voluntary and Nonprofit Organizations* 21 (1) (2010): 22–40. www.jstor.org/stable/27928196. Accessed March 21, 2020.

[63] David Ricci, *The Transformation of American Politics: The New Washington and the Rise of Think Tanks* (Yale University Press, 1993), p. 3.

[64] Donald E. Abelson, "*Think Tanks in the United States*," in Diane Stone, Andrew Denham, and Mark Garnett (Eds.): *Think Tanks Across Nations: A Comparative Approach* (Manchester University Press, 1998), 107–126 (p. 107–108).

[65] Diane Stone, *Capturing the Political Imagination: Think Tanks and the Policy Process* (London, Frank Cass: 1996), pp. 2–3.

system of checks and balances in addition to the weak party order.[66] To put it differently, the US system of checks and balances allows one party to control the executive branch while the opposing party rules the legislative one. This allows think tanks to gain more importance in terms of influencing policymaking through marketing their ideas and offering their expertise, especially in a political system where political parties play an insignificant role in terms of providing policy recommendations.

Despite the fact that it is difficult to establish a causal relationship between think tanks' recommendations and foreign policy decision making, Abelson claims that researchers can draw some important conclusions on the role of think tanks in the political decision making through finding some connections between think tanks' policy recommendations and the policies adopted by decision makers.[67] In so doing, scholars use some helpful indicators. These include media presence, congressional testimonies, the number of book sales, consultations with government departments and agencies as well as the fact that some think tanks' former fellows work as high-ranking officials in US administrations.[68]

According to McGain, not all of these indicators are to be considered "impact" indicators. He differentiates between four types of indicators: Resource, utilization, output, and impact.[69] First, resource indicators refer to, first and foremost, the capacity to hire and maintain pioneer academicians who carry out objective research and produce opportune and insightful analyses. Resource indicators also include the ability to retain stable and important funding as well as to maintain close and reliable contacts with decision makers, academic communities and the media.

Second, utilization indicators include qualitative and quantitative citations, presence in the media, web hits, hearings in legislative and executive entities, official meetings, book sales, consultations by members of

---

[66] Richard S. Katz, *Politische Partein in den Vereinigten States. Fokus Amerika Der Friedrich- Ebert-Stiftung*, (Washington, DC, 2007), 7.

[67] Abelson, think tanks in the quintes States, 1998.

[68] Martin Gehlen, *Politikberafung in den USA. Der Einflub Der Think Tanks AUI die amerikanische Sozialpolitik* (Frankfurt, 2005), pp. 35–36.

[69] McGann G. James, 2017. *Global Go To Think Tanks Index Report* (University of Pennsylvania, 2018), 34. Accessed February 15, 2019, https://repository.upenn.edu/cgi/viewcontent.cgi?article=1012&context=think_tanks.

1 INTRODUCTION   23

Congress and government departments/agencies, the number of participants in conferences and seminars organized by each think tank, and the number of references to their research and analyses in high-ranked scholarly sources.

Third, output indicators refer to the quantity and quality of policy recommendations, the number of publications produced, media interviews conducted, conferences, seminars, and briefings organized, and the number of nominations for highly ranked government posts among their staff.

Last but not least, impact indicators focus on the policy recommendations that are adopted or taken into consideration by decision makers, the number of advisory posts held to political parties and political candidates, awards granted, publications in academic journals, the number of subscribers and website visits, and the ability to question the ordinary knowledge and conventional operating strategies of policymakers.

The Multiple-Streams Theory
The Multiple-Streams theory was developed by John W. Kingdon in his book *Agendas, Alternatives and Public Policies*.[70] Kingdon argues that the process of establishing policies has three distinctive and independent streams which would converge to form the policy agenda. According to Kingdon, think tanks play a key role in these streams resulting in influencing the policy agenda through marketing their ideas to policymakers. The theory's streams are: The Problem Stream, the Policy Stream, and the Political Stream.

First, the Problem Stream refers to the type of issues under discussion in a particular society. These include but not limited to politics, science, technology, diplomacy, economy, and education. The relevant chapter's problem stream deals with US foreign policy in the Middle East and North Africa.

Second, the Policy Stream focuses on the quality of professional research and ideas produced by think tanks. Moreover, it copes with the extent to which these ideas attract the attention of policy makers. The chapter on think tanks examines the US think tanks' ability to attract US Presidents' attention pertaining to US foreign policy in the MENA

---

[70] John W. Kingdon, *Agendas, Alternatives, and Public Policies* (Boston: Little Brown, 2010).

area through prospective connections between think tanks' policy recommendations and the Presidents' foreign policy decisions from Clinton to Obama.

Third, the Political Stream mainly focuses on the direct relationship between think tanks and the government, especially the think tanks' personnel who are recruited to serve in different branches of government. For the purpose of the chapter on think thanks, we focus on think tanks' high-ranking personnel who were recruited to serve in the three administrations, and whose posts relate to foreign and defense policies.

This introductory chapter aimed at relating the definitions of foreign policy and the theoretical approaches of Foreign Policy Analysis (FPA) to the book's units of analysis which constitute the focus of the following chapters; namely, media, public opinion, interest groups, and think tanks. Chapter I explained the conceptual and theoretical frameworks that bind all of these non-state actors together in relation to their impact on foreign policy making. The following chapters discuss the role of the aforementioned non-state actors on initiating and shaping US foreign policy making in the MENA area through describing and analyzing their interactions with the executive power. The analysis starts with the media followed by the public opinion, interest groups, and think tanks.

CHAPTER 2

The Media and US Foreign Policy in the MENA Area: From the *War on Terror* to the *Arab Spring*

This chapter examines the impact of US media on US foreign policy in the Middle East and North Africa from the inception of the *war on terror* to the *Arab Spring*. We analyzed presidential rhetoric and media coverage of major events pertaining to the *war on terror* and the *Arab Spring* in order to assess the impact of US media on US foreign policy in the region.

To examine the direction of influence between policymakers and media, researchers have used a combination of qualitative and quantitative methodologies, especially content analyses of media coverage and interviews with policymakers. This chapter does not use interviews for two reasons. First, as a researcher in a Moroccan university, it is very difficult to have access to US policymakers. Second, interviewing policymakers on such critical issues as the *war on terror* may raise questions of the validity and reliability of answers. These answers are more likely to reflect how policymakers want to be recalled rather than how they really made their policies pertaining to the *war on terror*.

We used a combination of quantitative and qualitative methods. The qualitative method focuses on reviewing main events of the *war on terror* and the *Arab Spring* as well as the way American Presidents frame these events in their speeches. Additionally, we relied on general media frames of major events. As for the quantitative method, I made use of some statistical data of media effects, which are based on national surveys.

© The Author(s), under exclusive license to Springer Nature Switzerland AG 2024
F. Touzani, *Marketing US Foreign Policy in the MENA Region*, Political Campaigning and Communication,
https://doi.org/10.1007/978-3-031-45143-0_2

26 F. TOUZANI

THE PRESIDENTIAL DISCOURSE FROM 9/11 TO THE ARAB SPRING: FROM A RHETORIC OF FEAR TO A RHETORIC OF DEMOCRACY

The *war on terror* and the *Arab Spring* coincided with the presidencies of George W. Bush and Barack Obama. This chapter analyzes their speeches pertaining to US foreign policy in the MENA area from 2001 to 2013 in order to examine the extent to which their rhetoric set the media's agenda.

George W. Bush and the Rhetoric of Fear in the Post-9/11 Era: Setting the Agenda for the Media

The post-9/11 era was characterized by an overwhelming shock and fear taking into consideration the lamentable human losses. Bush started his campaign to sell the *war on terror* the day after the attacks in an address to the nation in which his discourse focused on accentuating Americans' fear through describing the attacks as "acts of war" and warning Americans stating "we're facing a different enemy than we have ever faced. This enemy hides in shadows and has no regard for human life".[1] In the same speech, Bush declared that America "will use all resources to conquer the enemy where they hide" without mentioning any specific targets. Few days after the attacks, an opinion poll showed that 79% of Americans considered these events as "acts of war".[2] Another post-9/11 poll showed that 75% of Americans were in favor of using force against a country where those involved in the attacks lived even if the country itself does not have a role in the attacks.[3] The positive correlation between Bush's rhetoric and the results of opinion polls indicates that Bush's war campaign influenced the American public opinion or, at least, emphasized the fear that Americans had after the attacks.

---

[1] George Bush, "Remarks by the President in Photo Opportunity with the National Security Team," September 12, 2001, https://georgewbush-whitehouse.archives.gov/news/releases/2001/09/20010912-4.html. Accessed June 4, 2019.

[2] Polling Report, "CNN/USA Today/Gallup Poll," Polling Report, September 14–15, 2001, http://www.pollingreport.com/terror10.htm. Accessed June 3, 2019.

[3] Polling Report, "NBC News/Wall Street Journal Poll," Polling Report, September 15–16, 2001, http://www.pollingreport.com/terror10.htm. Accessed June 3, 2019.

2 THE MEDIA AND US FOREIGN POLICY IN THE MENA AREA ... 27

It was in this atmosphere of fear that George W. Bush made the case for *the war on terror* in his speech of September 20, 2001. The rhetoric of fear in this speech was used by Bush to serve many purposes. First, it was used to justify the choice of Afghanistan and his targets of Al Qaeda, Taliban, and Osama Ben Laden:

> The leadership of al Qaeda has great influence in Afghanistan and supports the Taliban regime in controlling most of that country. In Afghanistan, we see al Qaeda's vision for the world.[4]

Bush continued to use the rhetoric of fear to legitimize his military intervention in Afghanistan:

> Thousands of these terrorists in more than 60 countries. They are recruited from their own nations and neighborhoods and brought to camps in places like Afghanistan where they are trained in the tactics of terror. They are sent back to their homes or sent to hide in countries around the world to plot evil and destruction.[5]

Second, the discourse of fear was utilized by Bush to justify his future preventive and long military interventions:

> Our nation has been put on notice: We are not immune from attack. We will take defensive measures against terrorism to protect Americans ... Our war on terror begins with al Qaeda, but it does not end there. It will not end until every terrorist group of global reach has been found, stopped, and defeated.[6]

Last but not least, Bush's use of fear also served an international purpose as Bush's infamous statement indicates:

---

[4] George Bush, "Address to a Joint Session of Congress and the American People," September 20, 2001, https://georgewbush-whitehouse.archives.gov/news/rel eases/2001/09/20010920-8.html. Accessed June 12, 2019.

[5] Ibid.

[6] Ibid.

28   F. TOUZANI

> Every nation in every region now has a decision to make: either you are with us or you are with the terrorists. From this day forward, any nation that continues to harbor or support terrorism will be regarded by the United States as a hostile regime.[7]

In such a moment of fear and uncertainty, American media adopted the Presidential rhetoric and supported Bush's *war on terror* through their TV coverage and newspaper editorials. Major American newspapers such as the *New York Times* (NYT), which is generally considered a liberal newspaper, and the *Washington Post* were very supportive of the war and Bush's choice of Al-Qaeda, Taliban, and Ben Laden as specific targets.[8] Other editorials frequently used the terms "evil", "corruption", and "state-sponsored terrorism" to describe Taliban and Al-Qaeda.[9] Interestingly enough, the ten largest American newspapers showed no opposition to the war and none of them predicted that it would fail from the 9/11 attacks to the inception of the war.[10] Furthermore, a study of the CNN coverage of the war in Afghanistan showed that 62% of the coverage dealt with "general military activity", while 17% only focused on human losses.[11] This shows that the Presidential framing of the war on terror through the use of the rhetoric of fear did set the agenda of the American media which played a crucial role in influencing the public opinion. To illustrate, Fig. 2.1 shows that paying attention to political media discourse significantly correlates with an increase in support of the war.[12]

In sum, we can say that George W. Bush took advantage of the atmosphere of fear that was already prevailing among Americans after the attacks of September 11. This fear was enhanced by the way he framed

---

[7] Ibid.

[8] See the *NYT's* editorial "War Without Illusions," September 15, 2001, https://www.nytimes.com/2001/09/15/opinion/war-without-illusions.html. Accessed June 12, 2019.

[9] Andrew Rojecki, "Rhetorical Alchemy: American Exceptionalism and the War on Terror," Political Communication 25 (2008): 67–88.

[10] Michael Ryan, "Framing the War against Terrorism: U.S. Newspaper Editorials and Military Action in Afghanistan," International Communication Gazette 66 (2004): 363–382.

[11] Amy E. Jasperson and Mansour O. El-Kikhia, "CNN and al Jazeera's Media Coverage of America's War in Afghanistan," in Framing Terrorism, Norris, Kern, and Just (2004): 113–132.

[12] Political-Media Effects on Public Opinion of War on Terror, November 2001-January 2002, Pew Research Center.

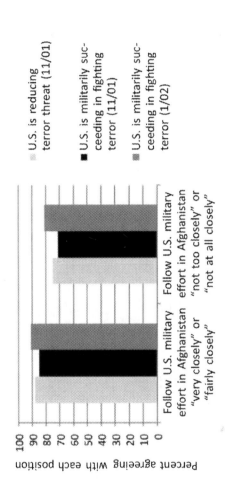

Fig. 2.1 Political-media effects on public opinion on the *War on Terror*: November 2001–January 2002 (*Source* Pew Research Center Surveys)

the attacks and the way he described and framed *the war on terror*. As a result, he was able to set the agenda of the US media which adopted his discourse and accepted using force in other countries starting with Afghanistan.

Iraq: Recycling the Discourse of Fear to Sell the War
The war in Afghanistan was followed by a campaign to sell the war in Iraq. In this campaign, George Bush focused on two main frames: Iraq's possession of Weapons of Mass Destruction (WMDs) and its regime's connection to terrorism. This large PR campaign started in 2002 and resulted in convincing Americans of the necessity to go to war in Iraq through enhancing the atmosphere of fear which was still an overwhelming feeling in the US.

To sell his war agenda internationally and give it a legal justification, Bush delivered a speech to the UN in September 12, 2002. In this speech, Bush described Saddam Hussein's regime as repressive and claimed that Iraq broke its commitments to the UN in terms of respecting human rights, supporting terrorist organizations, and possessing WMDs.[13] The speeches that followed reiterated the same frames. For example, he depicted Iraq as a "grave threat to peace" and warmed that this threat would become "worse with time".[14] He stated:

> If we know Saddam Hussein has dangerous weapons today—and we do— does it make any sense for the world to wait to confront him as he grows even stronger and develops even more dangerous weapon?[15]

Such alarming speeches increasingly increased in 2003 starting with the State of the Union address in which he referred to alleged Iraqi labs of biological weapons stating:

[13] George Bush, "Presidents Remarks at The United Nations General Assembly", September 12, 2002, https://georgewbush-whitehouse.archives.gov/news/releases/2002/09/20020912-1.html. Accessed June 14, 2019.

[14] George Bush, "President Bush Outlined Iraqi Threat", October 7, 2002, https://georgewbush-whitehouse.archives.gov/news/releases/2002/10/20021007-8.html. Accessed June 7, 2019.

[15] Ibid.

2 THE MEDIA AND US FOREIGN POLICY IN THE MENA AREA ... 31

The United Nations concluded in 1999 that Saddam Hussein had biological weapons sufficient to produce over 25,000 liters of anthrax—enough doses to kill several million people. He hasn't accounted for that material. He's given no evidence that he has destroyed it. The United Nations concluded that Saddam Hussein had materials sufficient to produce more than 38,000 liters of botulinum toxin—enough to subject millions of people to death by respiratory failure. ... He's given no evidence that he has destroyed it.[16]

This speech aimed at presenting Iraq as a real threat through conveying a message of uncertainty about its claim of not possessing biological weapons in order to influence the American and global public opinion and convince them of the necessity to wage war on Iraq. In a similar speech to the UN, Bush increased the degree of fear through warming against a possible development of nuclear weapons by Iraq:

Iraq employs capable nuclear scientists and technicians. It retains physical infrastructure needed to build a nuclear weapon.[17]

The same allegations were echoed by the Secretary of State Collin Powell in his speech to the UN of February 2003.[18]

To intensify the fear about Iraq, Bush frequently linked Saddam Hussein to Al Qaeda to remind Americans of September 11 attacks and maintain their fear. Interestingly enough, Bush's campaign to sell the war in Iraq started one day after the first September 11 anniversary. This indicates that the timing of the campaign was strategically chosen to further persuade Americans that Iraq was a genuine threat. In the speech of the first anniversary, Bush declared: "Saddam Hussein aids and protects terrorists, including members of al Qaeda".[19] Bush added:

---

[16] George Bush, "State of the Union Address," January 28, 2003, http://whitehouse.georgewbush.org/news/2003/012803-SOTU.asp, Accessed June 14, 2019.

[17] Bush, "Presidents Remarks at The United Nations General Assembly," September 12, 2002.

[18] Collin Powell, "US Secretary of State Address to the United Nations Security Council," February 5, 2003, https://www.theguardian.com/world/2003/feb/05/iraq.usa. Accessed June 25, 2019.

[19] Bush, "Presidents Remarks at The United Nations General Assembly," September 12, 2002.

Iraq and al Qaeda have had high-level contacts that go back a decade. Some al Qaeda leaders who fled Afghanistan went to Iraq. ... Iraq has trained al Qaeda members in bomb-making and poisons and deadly gases. And we know that after September the 11th, Saddam Hussein's regime gleefully celebrated the terrorist attacks on America.[20]

In addition to the alleged possession of WMDs, the development of nuclear weapons and links to Al Qaeda, Bush's campaign highlighted a third point about Saddam Hussein's regime. That is to say, its violations of human rights and its repressive attitude vis-à-vis its people. Bush denounced Saddam's

arbitrary arrest and imprisonment, summary execution, and torture by beating, burning, electric shock, starvation, mutilation, and rape. Wives are tortured in front of their husbands; children in the presence of their parents—all of these horrors concealed from the world by the apparatus of a totalitarian state.[21]

Bush emphasized his plan not to target civilians and directly addressed Iraqis saying:

We will deliver the food and medicine you need. We will tear down the apparatus of terror and we will help you to build a new Iraq that is prosperous and free. ... The tyrant will soon be gone. The day of your liberation is near.[22]

This emphasis on Saddam's human rights violations and his promises to Iraqis aimed at l combining the overwhelming message of fear with a message of hope; hope for Americans to overthrow one of the "supporters" of terror and hope for Iraqis to get rid of a dictator in order to establish a democratic regime in Iraq.

[20] Bush, "President Bush outlined Iraqi Threat," October 7, 2002.

[21] Bush, "Presidents Remarks at The United Nations General Assembly," September 12, 2002.

[22] George Bush, "Remarks by the President in Address to the Nation," March 17, 2003, https://georgewbush-whitehouse.archives.gov/news/releases/2003/03/200 30317-7.html. Accessed June 24, 2019.

It was later acknowledged that all these claims were deceitful. Saddam had no WMDs before the war and his regime had no connection to Al Qaeda. Melvin Goodman, a former CIA analyst, stated:

> The CIA and the intelligence community went too far in trying to accommodate the demands of the Bush administration... . The Bush administration, particularly Cheney, Rice, and Rumsfeld, made it clear what it wanted in the way of intelligence and kept sending reports back to be redone until it got the answers that it wanted. As a result, the CIA began to practice self-censorship and stopped distributing credible intelligence that argued against Iraq WMDs and links to al Qaeda.[23]

A further proof of Bush's deceptive information about Iraq came from the Iraq Study Group (ISG) which conducted a research about Iraq's WMDs after the war and concluded that Iraq was not a threat.[24] The head of ISG, David Kay, testified before Congress after the war and explained that Iraq demolished its chemical and biological programs in 1991 and its ability to rebuild its nuclear program faded away, especially after the UN inspectors' visits to Iraq in the 1990s.[25]

The US Media Coverage of the War in Iraq: A Reflection of Bush Propaganda

The presidential propaganda succeeded in selling the war in Iraq using misleading and distorted information about Iraq's alleged possession of WMDs and its links to Al Qaeda. Such information were favorably received by Americans because the Bush administration took advantage of the atmosphere of fear which was still prevailing after September 11. As a result, the Bush administration was able to set the agenda for the media which were significantly relying on official sources for their reporting.[26]

---

[23] Melvin Goodman, *Failure of Intelligence: The Decline and Fall of the CIA* (Lanham, MD: Rowman & Littlefield, 2008), 267–268.

[24] See the the full report of the Iraq Study Group. https://www.iraqsolidaridad.org/2006/docs/gei-1.pdf. Accessed June 24, 2019.

[25] "Transcript: David Kay at Senate Hearing," Carnegie Endowment for International Peace, January 28, 2004, https://carnegieendowment.org/2004/01/28/transcript-david-kay-at-senate-hearing-pub-14898. Accessed June 26, 2019.

[26] Lance Bennett, Regina G. Lawrence, and Steven Livingston, *When the Press Fails: Political Power and the News Media From Iraq to Katrina* (Chicago: University of Chicago Press, 2008).

34   F. TOUZANI

The Washington Post: A Total Reflection of Bush Rhetoric

The *Post's* coverage echoed the Bush discourse in terms of the pretexts given to justify the war in Iraq. To illustrate, the paper reported: "It is hard to imagine how anyone could doubt that Iraq possesses WMDs".[27] In a similar discourse, the same paper considered Iraq as "a threat not just to the United States, but to the global order".[28] The *Post* also echoed Bush's discourse on Iraq's alleged links to Al Qaeda. One of the paper's editorials warned that Saddam "shelters terrorists who have killed Americans and who would like to kill more".[29]

The *Post* also echoed Bush's rhetoric about establishing democracy in Iraq and liberating the Iraqis from Saddam's dictatorship. An editorial stated that the war in Iraq would "free the long-suffering Iraqi people, who have endured one of the cruelest and most murderous dictatorships of the past half-century".[30] In his evaluation of the *Washington Post's* front-page reporting from August 2002 to March 2003, Howard Kurtz, the former editor of the paper, concluded that the number of stories published by the paper exceeded 140 stories whose discourse echoed that of the Bush administration.[31] In contrast, an insignificant number of stories pointed to other motives such as US interests in Iraqi oil. Only two stories from June 2002 to March 2003 referred to oil as one of the

---

[27] "Irrefutable," *Washington Post*, February 6, 2003, https://www.washingtonpost.com/archive/opinions/2003/02/06/irrefutable/e598b1be-a78a-4a42-8e1a-c336f7a217f4/?noredirect=on&utm_term=.627653a2fb5c. Accessed June 26, 2019.

[28] "The Case for Action", February 5, 2003, https://www.washingtonpost.com/archive/opinions/2003/02/05/the-case-for-action/2ff69a62-a914-45ae-80b3-13f7997ef29e/?utm_term=.7f8e30642ac4. Accessed June 26, 2019.

[29] "The Perils of Passivity," *The Washington Post*, February 13, 2003, https://www.washingtonpost.com/archive/opinions/2003/02/13/the-perils-of-passivity/de03a4b3-7a84-4064-9fb2-8b283e4dc8b7/?utm_term=.2681ac833202. Accessed June 27, 2019.

[30] "First Strike Capability," *The Washington Post*, April 23, 2002, https://www.washingtonpost.com/archive/sports/2002/04/23/first-strike-capability/d10350c7-ed4d-4ec2-bca1-e225f183c126/?utm_term=.adc1e4765cad. Accessed July 1, 2019.

[31] Lisa Finnegan, *No Questions Asked: News Coverage Since 9/11* (Westport, CT: Praeger, 2006), 67.

2 THE MEDIA AND US FOREIGN POLICY IN THE MENA AREA ... 35

factors behind going to war in Iraq.[32] However, such a claim was discredited by the *Post* because this latter attributed it to members of the Iraqi regime which had no credibility among Americans during this period.

The New York Times: Reflecting Bush Rhetoric and Raising Concerns About the War

While the *Washington Post's* reflection of Bush's rhetoric can be justified because of the paper's clear conservative leanings and its connection to the Republican Party, the *Times* was supposed to represent an opposing view as it is known for its connection to the Democratic party. Surprisingly enough, this was not the case to a great extent. To illustrate, the editors of the paper positively commented on Bush's speech of September 11 first anniversary and praised the President for making a "compelling case" for "eliminating Iraq's unconventional weapons and insisting that Baghdad comply with the Security Council's longstanding disarmament orders".[33] A survey of the *Times'* editorials following Bush's speech of September 2002 showed that 73.6% of them implied that Saddam had or may have WMDs.[34]

Furthermore, the paper considered Iraq a "serious threat to international order".[35] As for the discourse on democracy, human rights as well as links to terrorism, the *Times* also reflected Bush's claims through emphasizing "Baghdad's brutal repression of minorities, its wholesale violations of human rights, and its tolerance for terrorism".[36] While hundreds of stories highlighted these claims, only four of them pointed out to Iraqi oil as one of the motives. Additionally, all of them were

---

[32] These Two Stories Are: Dan Morgan and David B. Ottaway, "In Iraqi War Scenario, Oil Is Key Issue," *Washington Post*, September 15, 2002, https://www.washingtonpost.com/archive/politics/2002/09/15/in-iraqi-war-scenario-oil-is-key-issue/ba43d2a9-abe5-4371-8f2c-445e262778a1/?noredirect=on&utm_term=.71b41bb2591b. Accessed July 8, 2019; Glenn Frankel, "Hussein Denies Charges in Interview, Oil Is U.S. Goal, Iraqi Leader Says," *Washington Post*, February 5, 2003, A17.

[33] "A Measured Pace on Iraq," *The New York Times*, September 14, 2002, https://www.nytimes.com/2002/09/14/opinion/a-measured-pace-on-iraq.html. Accessed July 1, 2019.

[34] Anthony DiMaggio, *Mass Media*, Mass Propaganda: Examining American News in the "War on Terror," (Lanham, MD: Lexington Books, 2008), 70.

[35] Ibid. "A Measured Pace on Iraq," *The New York Times*, September 14, 2002.

[36] "A Road Map for Iraq," *The New York Times*, September 18, 2002, https://www.nytimes.com/2002/09/18/opinion/a-road-map-for-iraq.html. Accessed July 1, 2019.

36 F. TOUZANI

attributed to Saddam's government which was already perceived as a threat in the US.[37]

Despite the fact that *the New York Times* echoed Bush's discourse about Iraq in terms of its possession of WMDs, its links to terrorism, and its repressive regime, the paper was cautious about supporting Bush's intention to invade this country unlike *the Washington Post* which expressed an unconditional support for Bush. The *Times* raised many concerns about the idea of going to war which included but not limited to potential human and financial American losses, the disadvantages of not having enough support from the UN and international allies in addition to the exhaustion of tactful means to topple Saddam's regime.[38]

It is important to point out that the choice of the *New York Times* and *the Washington Post* to illustrate the impact of Bush's rhetoric on the media is justified by the fact that they are considered as "agenda-setting" newspapers because they have an impact on other newspapers' reporting all over the US.

One of very few newspapers which offered a critical opinion of Bush's rhetoric was Knight Ridder with its prominent journalists Jonathan Landay and Warren Strobel. These journalists questioned Bush's claims about Iraq. However, their articles were neglected and marginalized because Bush's rhetoric dominated due to the atmosphere of fear that was already prevailing. It was only after the war that Landay and Warren

---

[37] These Stories Are: "Main U.S. Goal Is Oil Supply, Iraq Says," *New York Times*, September 3, 2002, https://www.nytimes.com/2002/09/03/world/main-us-goal-is-oil-supply-iraq-says.html; Julia Preston, "Hussein, in a Letter to General Assembly, Says Bush Wants to Control Mideast Oil," *New York Times*, September 20, 2002, https://www.nytimes.com/2002/09/20/world/threats-responses-baghdad-hussein-letter-general-assembly-says-bush-wants.html; "In Saddam Hussein's Words; It's for Oil," *New York Times*, September 20, 2002, https://www.nytimes.com/2002/09/20/world/threats-and-responses-in-saddam-hussein-s-words-it-s-for-oil.html?mtrref=www.google.com&gwh=0DD2BE721241BC712FCBEC5B51D43A9C&gwt=pay; John F. Burns, "Baghdad's View; Citing North Korea, an Iraqi Aide Says 'Oil and Israel,' Not Weapons, Spur the U.S.," *New York Times*, October 22, 2002, https://www.nytimes.com/2002/10/22/world/threats-responses-baghdad-s-view-citing-north-korea-iraqi-aide-says-oil-israel.html. All these articles were accessed on July 8, 2019.

[38] "Threats and Responses; Excerpts from House Debate on the Use of Military Force Against Iraq," *The New York Times*, October 9, 2002, https://www.nytimes.com/2002/10/09/us/threats-responses-excerpts-house-debate-use-military-force-against-iraq.html. Accessed July 3, 2019.

were recognized for their independent reporting and were offered the Raymond Clapper Memorial award.[39]

US Television News Networks: A Continuous Reflection of Bush Rhetoric

To begin with, it goes without saying that a news network such as the *Fox News* would undoubtedly and unsurprisingly mirror Bush's discourse due to its well-known conservative background. Not only did the *Fox News* reflect Bush's rhetoric on Iraq and advocate for war, but it harshly responded to voices opposing the war as well, which was very unique to this news network.[40]

Generally speaking, the Bush administration's rhetoric about Iraq dominated American TV networks. To illustrate, more than 75% of the guests who were invited to news programs before the war were associated with the government while only 1% of those guests represented the antiwar voice.[41] Similar findings were found after the war broke out. 71% of the guests who were invited to various news programs on CNN, ABC, PBS, NBC, and Fox supported the war while 10% only were against it.[42]

The critical reporting of the war briefly appeared in news network few months before the war started because it coincided with the Congressional debate on whether or not to authorize the President to go to war. Nevertheless, it was noted that this critical coverage decreased and faded away, especially after the Congress authorization of the war.[43] This means that journalists were biased and did not respect the principle of objectivity which is supposed to characterize the media, especially in a democracy. Ted Koppel, one of the ABC's hosts, stated:

---

[39] Lindsay and Strobel were granted this award by the Senate Press Gallery in February 5, 2004 for their independent coverage of the pre-war period.

[40] We found numerous examples of the *Fox'* responses to antiwar critics. These include but not limited to: Bill O'Reilly, "Should the U.S. Take Steps against Allies that Don't Support Iraqi Military Action?," The O'Reilly Factor, *Fox News*, February 26, 2003, 8 p.m.; Sean Hannity and Alan Colmes, "Interview with Neil Dobro, Steven Zunes," *Fox News*, February 17, 2003, 9 p.m.

[41] Timothy E. Cook, *Governing with the News: The News Media as a Political Institution* (Chicago: University of Chicago Press, 1998), 5–7.

[42] Ibid.

[43] Christopher Groshek, "Shifting Dissent: Media Coverage of the Decision to Go to War in Iraq," (International Communication Association Conference, New York, 2005).

38   F. TOUZANI

If the president says I'm going to war for reasons A, B, and C, I can't very well stand there and say, 'the president is not telling you the truth, the actual reason that he's going to war is some reason he hasn't even mentioned.'[44]

Koppel's statement suggests that attempting to challenge the official rhetoric could damage the journalist's reputation. Dan Rather from CBC news is a case in point.[45]

The most important conclusion to be drawn from the case study of the war in Iraq is that American presidents can set the media's agenda in terms of foreign policy decisions in the MENA area, especially in the early phase of conflicts. To put it differently, Bush was able to influence the media which mirrored his claims about Iraq to make his case to invade this country through taking advantage of the atmosphere of fear which prevailed after September 11.

The Failure and the Fall of Bush's Propaganda and the Shift in Media's Focus

The failure and the fall of Bush's propaganda were attributed to many factors. First, the fact that no WMDs were found in Iraq proved that Bush deceived Americans and lied to them. Second, the heavy human losses among Iraqi civilians and American forces raised a serious moral concern among the American public. Third, it was clear after the war that oil was a major motive behind going to Iraq, which was marginalized and not discussed in the pre-war period. Last but not least, the increase of violence in Iraq and the instability of the region resulted in questioning the international lawfulness of the war, which was not discussed much before.

The fall of Bush's propaganda is illustrated by a shift in the American public opinion about Iraq. By 2007, most Americans believed that the US made the wrong decision going to war and thought that the war was

[44] Ted Koppel, "Crisis Coverage and the Candy Bar Imperative," in *Feet to the Fire: The Media After 9/11*, ed. Kristina Borjesson (Amherst, NY: Prometheus Books, 2005), 31.

[45] For more information on Dan Rather's story, see Howard Kurtz, "Dan Rather to Step Down at CBS," *Washington Post*, November 24, 2004. https://www.washingtonpost.com/archive/politics/2004/11/24/dan-rather-to-step-down-at-cbs/3d8c6f2d-41a7-48b8-bd88-35181bfa0c7c/?noredirect=on&utm_term=.9a424fdf2d20.   Accessed July 7, 2019.

not going well.[46] In addition, the majority of Americans believed that Bush deliberately misled the US on WMDs and the US made a mistake sending in troops.[47] Furthermore, by 2004, most Americans supported a withdrawal of American troops from Iraq.[48]

The media played an important role in the shift in public opinion about the war, especially with their coverage of violent events and the increasing casualties among American troops despite Bush's continuous efforts to persuade Americans that military operations were making progress. This is illustrated by the percentage of Americans who were paying attention to the news about Iraq, which ranged from 60 to nearly 90% between December 2003 and December 2007 as shown in Fig. 2.2. Interestingly enough, this is the same period during which the majority of Americans expressed their opposition to the war as we explained in the previous paragraph. This suggests that there is a positive correlation between the increase in media coverage of violence in Iraq and the increase in Americans' opposition to the war.

The impact of media on the public opinion is illustrated by the percentage of Americans who knew the number of deaths among US forces by 2007. More than 60% of Americans surveyed knew that 3000 US forces were killed in Iraq by 2007.[49] This is mainly due to the media's focus on reporting violence and other critical events.

There were few important critical events which contributed in the shift in the American public opinion toward an increasing opposition to the war.

The Proof That Iraq Did Not Possess WMDs: The Decline of Bush Credibility

Many reports concluded that Iraq did not possess WMDs. The most important report appeared as early as 2004. It was authored by David Kay, the Chief US inspector, who stated that the US was "very unlikely to

---

[46] See Polling Report, "Pew Research Center survey," Polling Report, April 18–22, 2007, http://www.pollingreport.com/iraq6.htm. Accessed July 10, 2019.

[47] See "Iraq," Gallup, 2013, https://news.gallup.com/poll/1633/iraq.aspx. Accessed July 10, 2019.

[48] Ibid.

[49] Anthony R. DiMaggio, *When Media Goes to War: Hegemonic Discourse, Public Opinion, and the Limits of Dissent* (New York: Monthly Review Press, 2009), chap. 7.

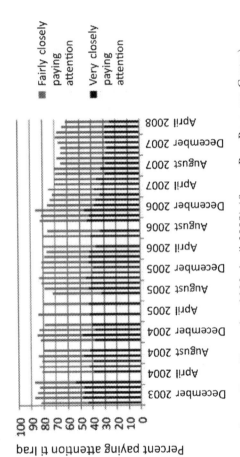

Fig. 2.2 Public attention to Iraq (December 2003–April 2008) (*Source* Pew Resource Center)

2 THE MEDIA AND US FOREIGN POLICY IN THE MENA AREA ... 41

find a large stockpiles of weapons".[50] The coverage of such reports influenced the public opinion. Figure 2.3 shows that Americans who followed the news on the absence of WMDs in Iraq were more likely to oppose the war and vote against the President in 2004.

The Abu Ghraib Prison Scandal: The Fall of Bush Humanitarian Rhetoric

The second important event contributing to the change in Americans' opinion about the war was the torture scandal of Abu Ghraib prison. This terrible event was first covered by the *New Yorker* and CBS followed by other news networks. The networks displayed horrible pictures of psychological, physical, and sexual abuses in addition to murders of Iraqi detainees by US interrogators and soldiers. The abuses were shockingly received worldwide and considered as severe violations to international humanitarian law.[51] Despite the fact that Bush denied his administration's responsibility of Abu Ghraib's scandal stating that those few soldiers are not representing the "democratic" American value. The fact that the US media did not show and report everything about this event including the images of torture marred the credibility of the war and weakened its humanitarian goals as claimed by Bush before. In fact, the Abu Ghraib scandal strengthened antiwar claims and increased the opposition to war.[52] Figure 2.4 shows that following the news on Abu Ghraib was associated with an increase in opposing the war.

Guantanamo Bay and the US Human Rights Abuses

Despite Bush's efforts to link Guantanamo's prisoners to terrorism in order to justify their detainment, the abuse and the torture of Guantanamo detainees aroused many controversies about the legality of their detainment and their rights to due process and fair trial. In addition

---

[50] "Kay: No Evidence Iraq Stockpiled WMDs," CNN, January 26, 2004, http://edition.cnn.com/2004/WORLD/meast/01/25/sprj.nirq.kay/, Accessed July 12, 2019.

[51] United Nations, "Convention Against Torture and Other Cruel, Inhuman or Degrading Treatment or Punishment," United Nations, December 10, 1984, https://www.ohchr.org/en/professionalinterest/pages/cat.aspx. Accessed July 12, 2019.

[52] Many pollsters associated the sudden decrease in Bush's public approval to Abu Ghraib scandal. See Jeffrey M. Jones and Joseph Carroll, "Deconstructing the Drop in Bush's Public Approval Rating," Gallup, June 1, 2004, https://news.gallup.com/poll/11872/deconstructing-drop-bushs-job-approval-rating.aspx. Accessed July 12, 2019.

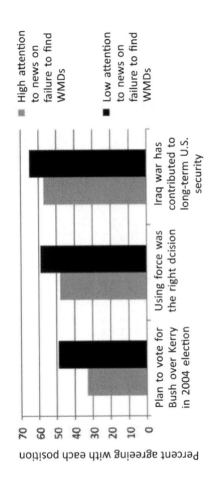

Fig. 2.3 The relationship between reporting on the absence of WMDs in Iraq and the Americans' opinion about the war (*Source* Pew Research Center Surveys [February 2004])

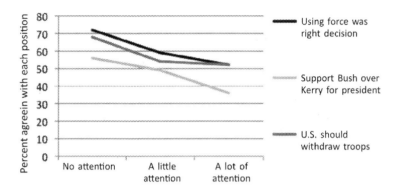

Fig. 2.4 The relationship between Abu Ghraib scandal and public opposition to war (*Source* Pew Research Center Surveys [April 2004])

to abusing the Koran by urinating on it, tearing it out, and writing abusive comments on its pages, the detainees were subjects to many types of physical, psychological, and sexual torture.[53] Surprisingly enough, nearly 80% of the detainees from 2002 to 2013 were set free with no charge.[54] Additionally, the US Supreme Court denied designating Guantanamo prisoners as "enemy combatants" twice in its rulings. The court commanded that the civilians must be offered civilian trials.[55]

These controversies obliged the Congress to hold hearings in 2005 to decide on the future of Guantanamo. These hearings were advocated for by Democrats who condemned the abuse and torture and considered the prison illegal according to international law and Geneva conventions. Figure 2.5 shows that reporting on Guantanamo was associated with a greater support to a withdrawal from Iraq. This also put Bush's humanitarian claim about war in Iraq into question.

---

[53] "Report Details Alleged Abuse of Guantanamo Bay, Abu Ghraib Detainees," *NewsHour*, PBS, June 18, 2008, https://www.pbs.org/newshour/nation/military-jan-jun e08-detainees_06-18. Accessed July 15, 2019.

[54] Andrew O'Hehir, "Guantanamo: It's Obama's Disgrace Now," *Salon*, May 4, 2013, https://www.salon.com/2013/05/04/guantanamo_its_obamas_disgrace_now/. Accessed July 15, 2019.

[55] Linda Greenhouse, "The Supreme Court: Detainees; Access to Courts," *New York Times*, June 29, 2004, https://www.nytimes.com/2004/06/29/us/the-supreme-court-detainees-access-to-courts.html. Accessed July 15, 2019.

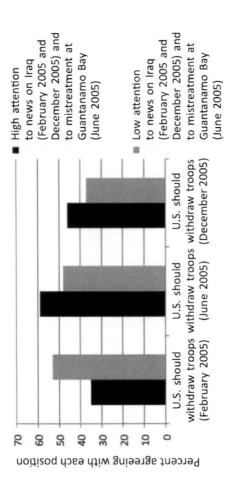

Fig. 2.5 The relationship between attention to news on Iraq and mistreatment at Guantanamo to Americans' support to a withdrawal from Iraq (*Source* Pew Research Center Surveys [February, June and December 2004])

2 THE MEDIA AND US FOREIGN POLICY IN THE MENA AREA ... 45

The Increasing Number of Human Losses Among US Soldiers

Furthermore, the increasing number of deaths among US troops also contributed to an increase in the opposition to the war. Reaching the 2000th death by October 25, 2005 was made a media event through an extensive coverage. In so doing, the media contributed to an increase in the opposition to the war. Figure 2.5 shows a positive correlation between a high attention to the news on Iraq and a greater support for a withdrawal from this country taking into consideration that the media's coverage started in October 2005.

The four aforementioned factors had a noticeable impact on shifting the American public opinion toward opposing the war and supporting a withdrawal. Indeed, the media played an important role in this shift through its coverage of the four events.

Iran: Reiterating the Presidential Rhetoric of Fear

The "*war on terror*" was Bush's major foreign policy goal after September 11 with his focus on the "axis of evil". In addition to Iraq, the "axis of evil" constitutes of Iran and North Korea. According to Bush, these countries represent a genuine threat to the US and its allies because they are keen on possessing WMDs.[56] Similar to what Bush did prior to the war in Iraq, Bush and Obama recycled the discourse of fear in their speeches to represent Iran as a threat to US and world security because of its alleged development of nuclear weapons.

Bush and the Perceived Iranian Threat

Bush's rhetoric on Iraq was similar to that of Iran. More particularly, the rhetoric on Iran focused on the country's alleged nuclear program. Bush's efforts to convey a message of fear about Iran coincided with two important events. First, there was an increasing tension between the IAEA inspectors and the Iranian government, which culminated in commanding Iran to stop its plans to enrich the uranium. Second, the 2005 Iranian elections resulted in electing Mahmoud Ahmedinejad as the President of Iran. Ahmedinejad was known for his antagonistic rhetoric toward the US. These two events facilitated Bush's efforts to present Iran as a threat to the US. Few months before the end of his second term, Bush alerted that:

---

[56] George Bush, "State of the Union Address," January 29, 2002, https://americanr hetoric.com/speeches/stateoftheunion2002.htm. Accessed July 16, 2019.

46   F. TOUZANI

Iran's actions threaten the security of nations everywhere. So the United States is strengthening our longstanding security commitments with our friends in the Gulf -- and rallying friends around the world to confront this danger before it is too late.[57]

Bush provided more details about these "actions" and described Iran as "the world's leading sponsor of terror". He also accused Iran of arming "the terrorist groups Hezboallah, Hamas and the Palestine Islamic Jihad" in addition to "refusing to be transparent about its nuclear programs and ambitions".[58]

The Media Coverage of Iran: An Overall Reflection of Bush Discourse

The media coverage of Iran during Bush terms was generally characterized by a reflection of Bush's discourse of fear through presenting Iran as a threat.

The *Washington Post* considered Iran a "principle threat" because of its "increasingly bold program to acquire the technology to produce nuclear weapons". Besides, the paper minimized the effectiveness of diplomatic means to deal with Iran.[59] Similarly, the *New York Times* editorials suggested that Iran's nuclear program had non-civilian purposes. The paper called the President to take necessary measures to prevent Iran from further developing its nuclear program.[60] Although the *Times* reported that diplomatic means did not succeed in deterring Iran from acquiring a nuclear weapon and criticized Bush for that, the paper, unlike the *Washington Post*, was not enthusiastic about the use of force. The paper called for a strategic evaluation of this option and warned that it would likely fail.[61]

---

[57] George Bush, "President Bush Discusses Importance of Freedom in The Middle East," January 13, 2008, https://georgewbush-whitehouse.archives.gov/news/releases/2008/01/20080113-1.html. Accessed July 17, 2019.

[58] Ibid.

[59] "Long Shots in Iran," editorial, *Washington Post*, July 9, 2003, A26.

[60] "Unraveling Iran's Nuclear Threats," *The New York Times*, May 9, 2003, https://www.nytimes.com/2003/05/09/opinion/unraveling-iran-s-nuclear-secrets.html. Accessed July 18, 2019.

[61] "Military Rumblings on Iran," *New York Times*, January 27, 2005, https://www.nytimes.com/2005/01/27/opinion/military-rumblings-on-iran.html. Accessed July 18, 2019.

2 THE MEDIA AND US FOREIGN POLICY IN THE MENA AREA ... 47

As far as television reporting is concerned, some research shows that TV networks were four times more likely to imply that Iran was trying to develop nuclear weapons than the counterargument.[62] In contrast, the IAEA reported that there is no credible evidence of Iran's development of nuclear weapons, which received far less attention from the US media.[63]

Barack Obama: A Temporary Change from Bush's Rhetoric

Unlike George Bush, who hinted at using force, Obama started his presidency with a more appealing rhetoric toward Iran. He addressed the Iranian leaders saying:

> My administration is now committed to diplomacy that addresses the full range of issues before us, and to pursuing constructive ties among the United States, Iran and the international community. This process will not be advanced by threats. We seek instead engagement that is honest and grounded in mutual respect. ... The United States wants the Islamic Republic of Iran to take its rightful place in the community of nations. You have that right—but it comes with real responsibilities, and that place cannot be reached through terror or arms, but rather through peace- full actions that demonstrate the true greatness of the Iranian people and civilization. And the measure of that greatness is not the capacity to destroy, it is your demonstrated ability to build and create.[64]

However, Obama's conciliatory tone did not last long. It soon changed to resemble Bush's rhetoric of fear, especially after the publication of reports by the IAEA and the Institute for Science and International Security. These reports warned that Iran's enriched uranium is sufficient to produce nuclear weapons.[65] Obama accused Iran of building a nuclear

[62] DiMaggio, Anthony. *When Media Goes to War*, 2009, 153–154.

[63] Ibid.

[64] Barack Obama, "A New Year, a New Beginning," March 19, 2009, https://obamaw hitehouse.archives.gov/blog/2009/03/19/a-new-year-a-new-beginning. Accessed July 17, 2019.

[65] David Albright, Paul Brannan, and Jacqueline Shire, "IAEA Report on Iran," *Institute for Science and International Security*, August 28, 2009, https://www.isis-online. org/publications/iran/Analysis_IAEA_Report.pdf. Accessed July 17, 2009.

48 F. TOUZANI

facility to enrich uranium. He warned that this would endanger US security.[66] Furthermore, despite Obama's threats to use force in case Iran pursued its uranium enrichment plan, he was committed to negotiations. This was criticized by Republicans who were leaning more toward using force.[67]

The Media Coverage of Iran: Different Responses to Obama's Agenda
The Washington Post: Criticizing Obama's Diplomatic Negotiations with Iran
The Post continued to express its strong belief in Iran as a threat during Obama's presidency. The paper was certain that Iran was increasingly close to acquiring a nuclear weapon and continuously warned Obama to intervene in order to block further development in Iran's nuclear plan before it was too late.[68] The *Post* was not hopeful about the UN's attempts to convince Iran to abandon its nuclear program and frequently reported that such attempts would very likely fail.[69]

The New York Times: Supporting Obama's Diplomatic Negotiations with Iran
The *Times'* coverage of Iran during Obama's presidency did not differ from the *Washington Post's* in terms of considering the country as a "threat". The two papers differ in how to deal with this "threat". The *Post* criticized Obama for engaging in negotiations with Iran. Furthermore, it advocated for a regime change as a means to prevent Iran from

[66] Barack H. Obama, "Statements by President Obama, French President Sarkozy, and British Prime Minister Brown on Iranian Nuclear Facility," The White House, September 25, 2009, https://obamawhitehouse.archives.gov/the-press-office/2009/09/25/statem ents-president-obama-french-president-sarkozy-and-british-prime-mi. Accessed 17, 2019.

[67] Barack Obama, " Remarks by the President at AIPAC Policy Conference," March 4, 2012, https://obamawhitehouse.archives.gov/the-press-office/2012/03/04/remarks-pre sident-aipac-policy-conference-0. Accessed July 17, 2019.

[68] "Running Out of Time to Stop Iran's Nuclear Program," Editorial, *Washington Post*, November 9, 2011, https://www.washingtonpost.com/opinions/running-out-of-time-to-stop-irans-nuclear-program/2011/11/09/gIQAiFDQ6M_story.html?utm_term=. 53636c98d113. Accessed July 21, 2019.

[69] "Iran at the Brink," Editorial, *Washington Post*, August 31, 2012, http://articles. washingtonpost.com/2012-08-30/opinions/35490315_1_supreme-leader-nuclear-facili ties-centrifuges. Accessed July 21, 2019.

acquiring nuclear weapons.[70] In contrast, the *Times* supported Obama's negotiations with Iran and was against the option of a military intervention.[71] However, the *Times* was very doubtful about whether the Iranian leaders would be willing to give up their nuclear program.[72]

US TV Networks: Mixed Responses to Obama's Agenda

Similar to major US newspapers, American television networks reflected Obama's perception of Iran as a "danger". However, some TV networks, such as the *Fox News,* opposed Obama on engaging in negotiations with Iran[73] while others such as MSNBC strongly supported Obama on the same issue.[74]

The presidential claims of both Bush and Obama were challenged by the head of the IAEA, Mohamed ElBaradei, who announced that there was "no credible evidence" about Iran's development of nuclear weapons.[75] The propagandistic Presidential rhetoric about Iran was similar to that of Iraq before the war when Bush claimed that Iraq presented a threat because of its alleged possession of WMDs. Despite the IAEA challenge of the presidential rhetoric, our analysis shows that the US media reflected the presidential perception of Iran as a "threat". However, it differed in how the presidents would deal with it.

---

[70] "More Half-Measures from Obama Administration on Iran," Editorial, *Washington Post*, November 22, 2011, https://www.washingtonpost.com/archive/politics/2002/09/15/in-iraqi-war-scenario-oil-is-key-issue/ba43d2a9-abe5-4371-8f2c-445e262778a1/. Accessed July 22, 2019.

[71] "Diplomacy on the Sidelines," Editorial, *New York Times*, April 6, 2009, https://www.nytimes.com/2009/04/06/opinion/06mon2.html?mtrref=www.google.com&gwh=25C3BCD6512538E8F5F9F5548F34FC15&gwt=pay. Accessed July 22, 2019.

[72] Ibid.

[73] Bill O'Reilly, "Pinheads and Patriots," The O'Reilly Factor, *Fox News*, September 25, 2009, 8:56 p.m.

[74] Rachel Maddow, The Rachel Maddow Show, MSNBC, December 27, 2011, 9:00 p.m.

[75] Julian Borger and Richard Norton-Tylor, "No Credible Evidence of Iranian Nuclear Weapons, Says UN Inspector", *The Guardian*, September 30, 2009, https://www.theguardian.com/world/2009/sep/30/iranian-nuclear-weapons-mohamed-elbaradei. Accessed July 18, 2019.

50 F. TOUZANI

The Impact of the Presidential Discourse and the Media on Americans
Figure 2.6 shows that the large majority of Americans had very unfavorable image of Iran and believed that it was developing nuclear weapons between 2006 and 2011. However, about 20% only believed that the US should pursue a military action. The US media played an important role in shaping the American public opinion because Americans are very unlikely to seek information about Iran from non-American media outlets.

The Iran case study resembles that of Iraq in terms of using the rhetoric of fear by both Bush and Obama. The use of such rhetoric by both presidents was effective and efficient in setting the US media's agenda through framing Iran as a "threat". As a result, the US media adopted the presidential rhetoric which focused on presenting Iran as a "danger". While the large majority of US media reflected the Presidents' perception of Iran as a "threat", they differed in how to cope with Iran's nuclear program. The media representing the conservative view were advocating for a military intervention while those representing the liberal view were leaning toward supporting negotiations and diplomatic means.

The Arab Spring *and the Change in Presidential Discourse*[76]
The Arab uprisings resulted in a change in the presidential discourse about the region from a discourse of fear to a discourse of democracy. This change in discourse can be attributed to two major factors. First, the impact of the rhetoric of fear declined owing to the negative repercussions of the wars in Afghanistan and Iraq. These repercussions include the fact that no WMDs were found in Iraq as well as the increase in human losses among American troops and civilians.

The second factor is the Arab uprisings. These events obliged Obama to stray from a long American support of repressive regimes in the MENA area because of the persistent and widespread protests of Arab masses in most countries in the region. These protests aimed at achieving social justice and equality. The protests resulted in regime change in Tunisia, Egypt, Libya, and Yemen few months only after the start of the uprisings. This is in addition to the initiation of political reforms in other countries.

---

[76] The *Arab Spring* started with demonstrations almost all over the MENA region. We chose the Egyptian and Libyan uprisings as cases studies because they were the most covered in Media and resulted in a regime change.

2 THE MEDIA AND US FOREIGN POLICY IN THE MENA AREA ... 51

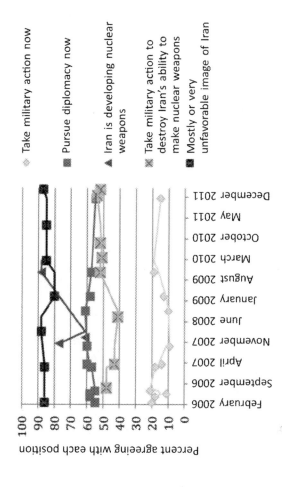

Fig. 2.6 Public opinion on Iran (February 2006–December 2012) (*Sources* CNN, NBC News/Wall Street Journal, Gallup and CBS News surveys)

52   F. TOUZANI

The Arab uprisings proved that Arabs and Muslims aspire to democracy and can peacefully and civically protest to achieve their goals. In fact, the uprisings challenged the orientalist discourse and the theory of "clash of civilizations", which dominated the American view of the Arab and Muslim world in the post-September 11 era. Such a discourse depicts Muslims and Arabs as anti-democratic, violent, exotic, and excessively passionate.[77]

The Egyptian Revolution and the Emerging Rhetoric of Democracy

The *Arab Spring* and its focus on democratic transitions in the Arab world coincided with Obama's first term. Obama's response to the Egyptian uprising was cautious, especially in the beginning and before the fall of Mubarak's regime. Few days after the start of the protest in January 25, 2011, Obama supported the Egyptians' rights to freedom of assembly, freedom of speech, and the freedom to have access to information.[78] However, his response to the idea of a regime change was very vague:

> An orderly transition must be meaningful, it must be peaceful, and it must begin now. The process must include a broad spectrum of Egyptian voices and opposition parties. It should lead to elections that are free and fair. And it should result in a government that's not only grounded in democratic principles, but is also responsive to the aspirations of the Egyptian people.[79]

Clearly, the rhetoric focused on democracy. However, there was no clear indication from Obama that Mubarak should step down. Rather, it seemed as if Obama was advising Mubarak to implement political reform to avoid his overthrow.

---

[77] For more information on the orientalist discourse, see Edward Said, *Orientalism* (New York: Vintage, 1979).

Said also wrote on the impact of the orientalist discourse on the public option in his book *Covering Islam: How the Media and the Experts Determine How We See the Rest of the World* (New York: Vintage, 1997).

[78] Barack Obama, "Remarks by the President on the situation in Egypt," February 1, 2011, https://obamawhitehouse.archives.gov/the-press-office/2011/02/01/remarks-president-situation-egypt. Accessed July 24, 2019.

[79] Ibid.

2 THE MEDIA AND US FOREIGN POLICY IN THE MENA AREA ... 53

The discourse supporting the Egyptians' democracy and freedoms sounds new and lacks credibility taking into consideration the longstanding US support of repressive regimes in the region including Hosni Mubarak's regime in Egypt, which ruled for more than thirty years. Obama responded to Mubarak's resignation in the same day saying "The people of Egypt have spoken, their voices have been heard, and Egypt will never be the same".[80]

Obama and the Egyptian Uprising: The Top Newsmaker in the US Media

Despite the Republican criticism of how Obama handled the situation in Egypt, Obama's discourse on Egypt dominated the US media mainly because of its focus on democratic rhetoric. In fact, Obama was considered "the top newsmaker" on Egypt in the US media.[81] Furthermore, a February 2011 survey showed that 66% of Americans described Obama's "handling of the situation in Egypt" as "good" or "very good".[82]

The New York Times and *the Washington Post* adopted Obama's rhetoric of democracy. The *Post* asked Mubarak to step down and encouraged Obama to reach out to the Egyptian military in order to urge it not to subdue the demonstrations using the $1 billion US aid to this institution as a pressure.[83] After Mubarak's overthrow, the *Times* asked Egyptians to "turn to the arduous work of building a new democratic order to replace the old authoritarian one.... The U.S. must be ready to now press for full democratic change".[84]

---

[80] Barack Obama, "Remarks by the President on the situation in Egypt," February 11, 2011, https://obamawhitehouse.archives.gov/the-press-office/2011/02/11/remarks-president-egypt. Accessed July 24, 2019.

[81] Pew Research Center, "The Fall of Mubarak and the Media," PEJ News Coverage Index, February 7–13, 2011, https://www.journalism.org/2011/02/12/pej-news-coverage-index-february-713-2011/. Accessed July 24, 2019.

[82] NBC News/Wall Street Journal Poll, Polling Report, February 14, 2011, https://www.pollingreport.com/work2.htm Accessed July 25, 2019.

[83] "The U.S. Needs to Break with Mubarak Now," Editorial, January 29, 2011, http://www.washingtonpost.com/wp-dyn/content/article/2011/01/28/AR2011012805399.html. Accessed July 24, 2011.

[84] "Egypt's Moment," Editorial, New York Times, February 11, 2011, https://www.nytimes.com/2011/02/12/opinion/12sat1.html?mtrref=www.google.com&gwh=C01DD94F912DE0CCDE6F3D87EF97D0A6&gwt=pay. Accessed July 24, 2011.

54 F. TOUZANI

The Egyptian Military Coup and Obama's Loss of Control

The 2012 elections following the overthrow of Mubarak were considered the first free and transparent elections in the history of Egypt in more than 30 years. These elections resulted in electing Mohammed Morsi from the Muslim Brotherhood as the President of Egypt. Few months after Morsi's election, Egyptians came back to the streets to express their dissatisfaction with the economic and social situation in the country. The Egyptian military took advantage of this situation and organized a *coup* which resulted in overthrowing Morsi and putting him in prison in July 2013. The imprisonment of Morsi was followed by repressive attacks by the Egyptian military on his followers, which resulted in hundreds of deaths and thousands of injuries among protestors. Thus, Egypt returned to authoritarianism and military rule and the dream of democracy faded away.

Obama's immediate response to the *coup* was very limited. More importantly, he did not accept to call the military intervention against Morsi a "*coup*" and stated that he is "deeply concerned" by the removal of Morsi. This is in addition to a very vague rhetoric which calls the military to return to democracy.[85] Surprisingly enough, Obama continued to provide aid to the Egyptian military despite killing hundreds of protestors and injuring thousands.

The Egyptian case study shows that the Egyptian uprising set Obama's agenda. Obama's rhetoric of democracy dominated the American media. However, this dominance was limited to early 2011 which coincided with the outbreak of the uprising and the overthrow of Hosni Mubarak. The US media's coverage of the uprising and the overthrow of Mubarak was very significant and reflected Obama's discourse of democracy. In contrast, the rise of the Muslim Brotherhood in power and Obama's limited responses to the military *coup* against Morsi influenced the media's coverage of Egypt from the second half of 2011 to 2013. Additionally, the attention was redirected to emerging issues in the region in 2012 and 2013, especially the civil war in Syria and the attacks on US embassy in Libya.

---

[85] E Obama, "Statement by BARACK Obama on Egypt," July 3, 2013, https://obamawhitehouse.archives.gov/the-press-office/2013/07/03/statement-president-barack-obama-egypt. Accessed July 25, 2019.

2 THE MEDIA AND US FOREIGN POLICY IN THE MENA AREA ... 55

The Libyan Uprising and the American Intervention in Libya

Unlike the Egyptian uprising, the Libyan one was armed. It started in February 17, 2011 and involved Muammar Gaddafi's forces against those of the rebels who were poorly armed and less numerous. The increasing number of deaths among civilians and the limited access to water in some Libyan areas raised an international humanitarian concern. Under the humanitarian cover, the NATO imposed a no-fly zone and a naval blockade on Gaddafi's forces in March. Additionally, the US-NATO forces participated in a series of attacks targeting Gaddafi's forces. As a result, more civilians were murdered, which was criticized by human rights organizations despite the fact that the attacks were justified by humanitarian concerns. The civil war and the US-NATO intervention ended with killing Gaddafi and the UN recognition of the rebels' National Transitional Council as Libya's legal representative in September 15, 2011.

Obama justified the US intervention in Libya by his concern for human lives:

> we saw the prospect of imminent massacre; we had a mandate for action, and heard the Libyan people's call for help. Had we not acted along with our NATO allies and regional coalition partners, thousands would have been killed.[86]

Furthermore, Obama continued his adoption of the democratic rhetoric with the Libyan crisis: "When Gaddafi inevitably leaves or is forced from power, decades of provocation will come to an end, and the transition to a democratic Libya can proceed".[87]

Obama's exclusive focus on the rhetoric of democracy and his concern for human rights in Libya with no mention of US interest in the Libyan oil may prompt one to question the credibility of his discourse, especially after the long-standing US silence about Gaddafi's repressive regime, except when the Libyan leader tried to strengthen his relations with the Soviet Union and challenged the US capitalist economic system. An important part of Gaddafi's challenge of US free market was making the

---

[86] Barack Obama, " Remarks by the President on the Middle East and North Africa," May 19, 2011, https://obamawhitehouse.archives.gov/the-press-office/2011/05/19/remarks-president-middle-east-and-north-africa. Accessed July 26, 2011.

[87] Ibid.

56   F. TOUZANI

exploitation of the Libyan oil very difficult and costly for foreign corporations. Thus, the US opposition to Gaddafi's regime was rarely driven by its human rights transgressions. Indeed, the US strategic interest in the region's oil has always been a fundamental characteristic of US foreign policy.

The Media Coverage of the Libyan Crisis: A reflection of Obama's Rhetoric

The US media reflected Obama's humanitarian and democratic discourse. To illustrate, the *New York Times* considered Gaddafi a "Butcher" and advocated for a military intervention: "We have no doubt that Gaddafi will butcher and martyr his own people in his desperation to hold on to power. He must be condemned and punished by the international community".[88] A study of 56 *Times* stories about Libya in 2011 revealed that the newspaper was more than five times as likely to focus on humanitarian rhetoric in comparison to other themes such as US interests in Libya's oil.[89] In fact, the *Washington Post* had the same viewpoint.[90]

While most TV networks supported Obama's intervention in Libya, very few criticized it for different reasons. For example, the *Fox News* criticized Obama for not toppling Gaddafi earlier and not using enough military resources in the intervention.[91] The media's effects on the US public opinion were significant. According to a Pew survey on Libya conducted in March 11, Americans who followed the news on Libya were more likely to agree with a US military intervention.[92]

---

[88] "Libya's Butcher," Editorial, *New York Times*, February 22, 2011, https://www.nyt imes.com/2011/02/23/opinion/23wed2.html, Accessed August 5, 2019.

[89] Anthony R. DiMaggio, "Propaganda for 'Justice': Flattering the State on Libya and Bin Laden," Truthout, May 26, 2011, http://truth-out.org/index. php?option = com_ k2&view = item&id = 1278:propaganda-for-justice-flattering-the- state-on-libya-and-bin-laden. Accessed July 27, 2019.

[90] See "Obama Demands Pull-back of Libya Troops, Tripoli Declares Cease Fire," *Washington Post*, March 18, 2011, https://www.washingtonpost.com/?utm_term=.117 788c574f2. Accessed July 27, 2019.

[91] "Shock: Hannity Would Support Action in Libya if McCain Were President," Media Matters for America, March 24, 2011, https://www.mediamatters.org/video/2011/03/ 24/shock-hannity-would-support-action-in-libya-if/177935. Accessed July 28, 2019.

[92] Pew Research Center Survey, "Public Wary of US Military Intervention in Libya," March 23, 2011, https://www.pewresearch.org/fact-tank/2011/03/23/public-wary-of-u-s-military-intervention-in-libya/. Accessed July 28, 2019.

2 THE MEDIA AND US FOREIGN POLICY IN THE MENA AREA ... 57

The death of Gaddafi was celebrated by Obama and the US media. Obama seized this opportunity to reproduce the discourse of democracy and human rights. He stated that Gaddafi's death:

> marks the end of a long and painful chapter for the people of Libya, who now have the opportunity to determine their own destiny in a new and democratic Libya.... For four decades, the Qaddafi regime ruled the Libyan people with an iron fist. Basic human rights were denied.[93]

The *Times* reported that Gaddafi's death allowed Libyans "to build their stable and peaceful democracy".[94] The *Washington Post* commented on the future of Libya and the entire region stating that "Libya's stabilization under a democratic government could help tip the broader wave of change in the Arab Middle East toward those favoring freedom".[95]

Obama's Rhetoric of Democracy: From an Incontestable Success to a Shaky One
The Egyptian and Libyan case studies revealed that Obama was successful in fostering public support for his foreign policy in the MENA area. The US media played an important role in shaping the public opinion through adopting and mirroring Obama's rhetoric of democracy and human rights. The firmness of this success started to shake after the attack on US facilities in Benghazi and the rise of the Syrian uprising.

The Bombings in Benghazi: The Fall of Obama's Rhetoric and the Rise of the Media
The US embassy in Benghazi as well as the CIA annex in the same city were attacked in September 11, 2012. These attacks coincided with the eleventh anniversary of 9/11. The Benghazi attacks resulted in four

---

[93] Barack Obama, "Remarks by the President on the Death of Muammar Qaddafi," October 20, 2011, https://obamawhitehouse.archives.gov/the-press-office/2011/10/20/remarks-president-death-muammar-qaddafi. Accessed July 27, 2019.

[94] Neil Macfarquhar, "An Erratic Leader, Brutal and Defiant to the End," *New York Times*, October 20, 2011, https://www.nytimes.com/2011/10/21/world/africa/qaddafi-killed-as-hometown-falls-to-libyan-rebels.html. Accessed July 27, 2019.

[95] "For Post-Gaddafi Libya, 'Now the Hard Part Begins,'" editorial, *Washington Post*, October 20, 2011, https://www.washingtonpost.com/opinions/for-post-gaddafi-libya-now-the-hard-part-begins/2011/10/20/gIQAzSRg1L_story.html. Accessed July 27, 2019.

58 F. TOUZANI

deaths and ten injuries among Americans including US Ambassador to Libya, Christopher Stevens. Three days later, Al-Qaeda announced their responsibility for the attacks and declared that they were a revengeful response to the death of Abu Yahya Al-Libi, Al Qaeda member who was killed in Pakistan by the US few months before Benghazi attacks.

Obama and His Controversial Response to Benghazi Attacks

The first responses from Obama described the attacks as "acts of terror" and promised to bring the attackers to justice.[96] The US media criticized Obama for not guaranteeing the safety of the US diplomats. The criticism increased after publishing the results of a Congressional investigation which was mostly led by Republicans. The investigation concluded that senior officials at the US State Department continuously decreased the number of security staff in Benghazi embassy despite their knowledge of the high security risks facing US diplomats there.[97] Obama described the controversy raised by the Congressional report as a political "sideshow" and criticized Republicans for politicizing the issue.[98]

Media Coverage of Benghazi Attacks and Its Impact on Obama's Credibility

The criticism to Obama's response to Benghazi attacks came mainly from right-wing conservative media which echoed Republican criticism. To illustrate, the *Fox News* called Benghazi a "scandal" and criticized Obama for not promptly characterizing the attacks as "acts of terror". Additionally, the *Fox* criticized the President for not taking the necessary security

---

[96] Barack Obama, "Remarks by the President on the Death of US Embassy Staff in Libya," September 12, 2012, https://obamawhitehouse.archives.gov/the-press-office/2012/09/12/remarks-president-deaths-us-embassy-staff-libya. Accessed July 29, 2019.

[97] This was a joint report by five Congressional committees: Armed Services, Foreign Affairs, Intelligence, Judiciary, and Oversight & Government Reform. The report was titled "Progress Report on Benghazi Terror Attack Investigation," April 23, 2013, https://www.hsdl.org/c/progress-report-on-benghazi-terrorist-attacks-investigation/. Accessed July 29, 2019.

[98] "President Obama and British Prime Minister David Cameron Joint press Conference," May 13, 2012, https://m.youtube.com/watch?v=puwwLIhEysw. Accessed July 29, 2019.

2 THE MEDIA AND US FOREIGN POLICY IN THE MENA AREA ...   59

measures to protect the US diplomats.[99] It is important to note that the Obama administration initially referred to the attacks as "spontaneous protest against an anti-Muslim film".[100] Liberal media defended Obama and considered Benghazi a "manufactured scandal" which does not deserve much attention.[101]

The CNN's disclosure of Christopher Stevens' journal contributed in weakening Obama's rhetoric on Benghazi. Ambassador Stevens, who was murdered in Benghazi, criticized the defective security around the US diplomatic compound and warned against potential attacks from extremists in his journal.[102] The CNN's story placed Obama at a great disadvantage. In fact, Obama and his administration were sometimes incapable of controlling the US media's reporting, especially after the continuous coverage of congressional committee hearings on Benghazi. As a result, Obama's rhetoric was generally disfavored.

The media's coverage of Benghazi had a negative impact on Obama's credibility. Figure 2.7 shows that Americans who followed the news on Benghazi were more likely to disapprove of Obama's rhetoric and approve of the Republican one than those who do not follow the news. More specifically, those who followed the reporting on Obama's initial claim of "spontaneous protects" and Ambassador Stevens' request of more security were more likely to disapprove of Obama.[103]

The Syrian Uprising and Obama's Loss of Control
The Syrian uprising started in March 2011 with peaceful protests expressing discontent with Bashar al-Assad's regime and asking for his removal. The Syrian regime violently suppressed the protests, which

[99] Arthur Herman, "Three Key Questions on the Benghazi Scandal," *Fox News*, November 13, 2012, https://www.foxnews.com/opinion/three-key-questions-on-the-benghazi-scandal. Accessed July 30, 2019.

[100] Ibid.

[101] "There Were Meaningful Benghazi Lies After All," *MSNBC the Rachel Maddow Show*, May 17, 2013, http://www.msnbc.com/rachel-maddow-show/there-were-meaningful-benghazi-lies-afte/amp. Accessed July 30, 2019.

[102] "CNN Finds, Returns Journal Belonging to Late U.S. Ambassador," the CNN Wire Staff, September 23, 2019, https://edition.cnn.com/2012/09/22/world/africa/libya-ambassador-journal/index.html. Accessed July 23, 2019.

[103] Bruce Stokes, "The Whole World Is Watching," Pew Research Center, October 22, 2012, https://www.pewresearch.org/global/2012/10/22/the-whole-world-is-watching/. Accessed July 31, 2019.

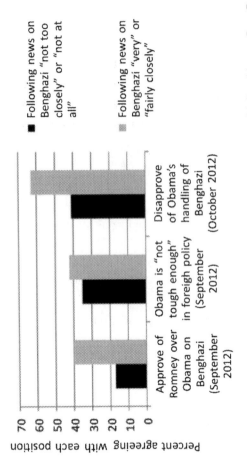

Fig. 2.7 The impact of the US media's coverage of Benghazi on Obama's credibility (*Source* Pew Research Center Survey [September and October, 2012])

2 THE MEDIA AND US FOREIGN POLICY IN THE MENA AREA ... 61

contributed to escalating the conflict to a civil war. This civil war was further escalated by the end of 2013 with the involvement of new actors. As a result, the war became more complicated, especially with the rise of fundamentalist groups such as ISIS which fought against Assad's regime. Assad's regime was militarily supported by Hezbollah and the Iranian government as well as Russia.

Obama: A Shaky Response to the Syrian Crisis

The first Obama's response to the Syrian uprising was laconic, especially with considering a potential US intervention in the conflict. In addition to his humanitarian rhetoric describing the human losses in the war as "heartbreaking", Obama expressed his opposition to a US military intervention in Syria provided that Assad does not use chemical and biological weapons in the war, which Obama called a "red line".[104]

In September 2013, the United Nations confirmed the use of chemical weapons in Syria without holding the Assad's regime accountable.[105] Obama took advantage of this report to launch a campaign aiming at gaining public support for a US military intervention against Assad's regime. Obama stated:

> *The* situation profoundly changed on August 21, when Assad's government gassed to death over a thousand people, including hundreds of children. The images from this massacre are sickening: Men, women, children lying in rows, killed by poison gas. Others foaming at the mouth, gasping for breath. A father clutching his dead children, imploring them to get up and walk. On that terrible night, the world saw in gruesome detail the terrible nature of chemical weapons, and why the overwhelming majority of humanity has declared them off- limits—a crime against humanity, and a violation of the laws of war.[106]

[104] Barack Obama " Remarks by the President at AIPAC Policy Conference," March 4, 2012, https://obamawhitehouse.archives.gov/the-press-office/2012/03/04/remarks-president-aipac-policy-conference-0, Accessed July 17, 2019.

[105] United Nations, "United Nations Mission to Investigate Allegations of the Use of Chemical Weapons in the Syrian Arab Republic," August 21, 2013, https://www.un.org/zh/focus/northafrica/cwinvestigation.pdf Accessed August 30, 2019.

[106] Barack Obama, "Remarks of the President in an Address to the Nation on Syria," September 10, 2013, https://obamawhitehouse.archives.gov/the-press-office/2013/09/10/remarks-president-address-nation-syria. Accessed August 1, 2019.

Despite the use of humanitarian rhetoric focusing on protecting civilians, gaining public and Congressional support for an intervention in Syria seemed challenging for Obama, especially with the destructive effects of the war in Iraq and the WMDs lie based on which George Bush invaded this country. Members of Congress who opposed the US intervention questioned its effectiveness and argued that it would escalate the conflict further and lead to more deaths. Furthermore, the opponents of a US intervention referred to the UN report which did not hold Assad's regime liable for using chemical weapons. This undermined Obama's argument against the Assad's regime, which was mainly based on declassified intelligence information.

As a response to the strong oppositional argument, Obama declared that the strikes on Syria would be temporary and precise and warned that chemical weapons may end in terrorists' hands.[107] The strong public and Congressional opposition to Obama's plan to intervene in Syria pushed him to refrain from the idea and engage in an agreement with the Syrian government. The agreement would be carried out by the UN with Russia as intermediary. According to the agreement, the Syrian regime must dismantle its chemical weapons by mid-2014.[108] Obama's retreat from a potential intervention in Syria illustrates the power of the system of checks and balances in the American political system as well as the power of the US public opinion.

The Thriving of the US Media

The US media coverage of the Syrian case combined sympathetic and unfavorable messages to Obama's rhetoric. The *Washington Post* criticized Obama for not taking a unilateral military action in Syria and choosing to engage in a multilateral diplomatic solution to disarm Assad through the UN and Russia.[109] Nevertheless, the *Post* was supportive of Obama's idea to provide the Syrian insurgents with weapons to help them overthrow

---

[107] Ibid.

[108] "UN Security Council Agrees to Rid Syria of Chemical Weapons, Endorses Peace Process," *UN News*, September 27, 2013. https://news.un.org/en/story/2013/09/451502-un-security-council-agrees-rid-syria-chemical-weapons-endorses-peace-process. Accessed August 1, 2019.

[109] "A Scapegoat for Syria?" Editorial, *Washington Post*, July 6, 2012. https://www.washingtonpost.com/opinions/a-scapegoat-for-syria/2012/07/06/gJQA4xbeSW_story.html. Accessed August 2, 2019.

2 THE MEDIA AND US FOREIGN POLICY IN THE MENA AREA ... 63

Assad.[110] Following the chemical attacks, the *Post* encouraged Obama to take a military action and warned against a potential use of these weapons to attack US targets in the region.[111]

The *New York Times* provided a more balanced view and was skeptical of the usefulness of a military action. The paper held both the revolutionists and the Assad's regime responsible for the critical humanitarian situation in Syria.[112] Unlike the *Post*, the *Times* praised Obama for resisting a military action in the beginning of the conflict as well as for providing the insurgents with weapons.[113] As a response to Obama's suggestion of a military action following the chemical attacks, the *Times* criticized Obama's suggestion, especially with the strong national and international opposition.[114]

The coverage of the main news channels was similar to that of the major newspapers in terms of conveying a combination of supportive and disapproving messages to Obama's discourse. The Fox News reported that the use of chemical weapons was Assad's responsibility. Consequently, it advocated for a US military intervention to punish him for trespassing the "red line".[115] Although MSNBC mirrored Obama's belief of Assad's

---

[110] "U.S. Policy on Syria Still Lacks Coherence," Editorial, *Washington Post*, May 1, 2013 https://www.washingtonpost.com/opinions/us-policy-on-syria-still-lacks-coherence/2013/05/01/dbda6cfc-b27b-11e2-bbf2-a6f9e9d79e19_story.html?utm_term=.9b0a2aab6a04. Accessed August 2, 2019.

[111] "U.S. Must Act Against Crimes Against Humanity," Editorial, *Washington Post*, August 30, 2013. https://www.washingtonpost.com/opinions/us-must-act-against-crimes-against-humanity/2013/08/30/dad67a26-1199-11e3-b4cb-fd7ce041d814_story.html?utm_term=.27155055f17b. Accessed August 30, 2019.

[112] "Wrong:Ways to Fight Assad," editorial, *New York Times*, March 20, 2012, https://www.nytimes.com/2012/03/21/opinion/wrong-ways-to-fight-bashar-al-assad.html?mtrref=www.google.com&gwh=A47480E9408C44B6F3A2BF8E4D0B0D5D&gwt=pay&assetType=REGIWALL. Accessed August 2, 2019.

[113] "Measured Approach to the Syrian Crisis," Editorial, *New York Times*, November 30, 2012, https://www.nytimes.com/2012/12/01/opinion/a-measured-approach-to-the-syrian-crisis.html. Accessed August 2, 2019.

[114] "After Arming the Rebels, Then What?" Editorial, *New York Times*, June 14, 2013, https://www.nytimes.com/2013/06/15/opinion/after-arming-the-rebels-then-what.html. Accessed August 2, 2019.

[115] "Atrocities' Could Trigger Military Intervention in Syria, Joint Chiefs Chairman Warns," *Fox News*, May 23, 2012, https://www.foxnews.com/politics/atrocities-could-trigger-military-intervention-in-syria-joint-chiefs-chairman-warns. Accessed August 3, 2019.

responsibility for the chemical attacks, the news channel was not credulous of the utility of a US intervention.[116]

In brief, the media coverage of Syria generally reflected Obama's rhetoric in 2012 because of its emphasis on humanitarian discourse and Obama's initial opposition to a US military intervention. Despite this reflection, Obama's rhetoric was not appealing for Americans because most of them were not following the news on Syria in 2012. To illustrate, the percentage rarely reached 40% and nearly 70% stated that they paid "a little" or "no" attention to the news about Syria.[117]

The coverage changed in 2013 following the chemical attacks. It became increasingly critical of Obama's rhetoric because of his intention to militarily intervene in Syria. Therefore, Obama's military agenda declined as approximately 74% of Americans believed that a US military intervention in Syria would create a backlash against the US and its allies in the region.[118] Indeed, the US media played an important role in shaping the public opinion on Syria. According to Pew Research Center surveys, Americans who paid more attention to the news on Syria were more likely to reject Obama's military plan.[119] The Syrian case illustrated the importance of the media in shaping the public opinion, which contributed to deterring Obama from militarily intervening in Syria.

All in all, unlike the Egyptian and the Libyan cases in which Obama's rhetoric generally dominated the American media and gained public support for his foreign policy agenda in the MENA area, the Benghazi and the Syrian cases marked the beginning of a decline in presidential rhetoric and the thriving of other actors including the media.

This chapter discussed the impact of US media on US foreign policy in the MENA area from the inception of the *war on terror* to the *Arab Spring*. We examined presidential rhetoric and media coverage of major

[116] Chris Hayes, All In with Chris Hayes, MSNBC, June 14, 2013, 8 p.m. est. Rachel Maddow, The Rachel Maddow Show, MSNBC, June 13, 2013, 9 p.m. est; Ed Schultz, The Ed Show, MSNBC, May 12, 2013, 5 p.m. est.

[117] Bruce Stokes, "Americans on Middle East turmoil: Keep Us Out of It," Pew Research Center, December 14, 2012, https://www.pewresearch.org/global/2012/12/14/americans-on-middle-east-turmoil-keep-us-out-of-it/. Accessed August 4, 2019.

[118] Pew Research. Enter, "Public Opinion Runs Against Syrian Airstrikes," September 3, 2013, https://www.people-press.org/2013/09/03/public-opinion-runs-against-syrian-airstrikes/. Accessed August 4, 2019.

[119] Pew Research Center, September 2013 Political Survey, https://www.people-press.org/dataset/september-2013-political-survey/. Accessed August 4, 2019.

incidents relating to these events. The analyses revealed that the US Presidents are generally more successful in setting the media's agenda while the media are more likely to influence the public opinion. However, rarely do American media set the Presidents' agenda pertaining to US foreign policy in the MENA area. The following chapter examines the impact of another non-state actor on initiating or shaping US foreign policy in the region. That is to say, the public opinion.

CHAPTER 3

The US Public Opinion: A Marginal Impact on US Foreign Policy

This chapter assesses the role of US public opinion in shaping US foreign policy in the Middle East and North Africa during the period extending from Ronald Reagan's presidency to Barack Obama's. We analyzed presidential foreign policy decisions with a focus on US military interventions in the MENA region. We also examined the results of public opinion polls about the major events that coincided with the same period. The chapter's main purpose is to find out whether US public opinion has an impact on the Presidents' decisions to use force in the MENA area.

RONALD REAGAN AND US INTERVENTION IN LEBANON (1982–1984): A COMPLETE DISINTEREST IN THE AMERICAN PUBLIC OPINION

The Pre-1983 Bombings on US Marines: Reagan's Disinterest in the Public Disapproval of US Military Presence in Lebanon

After the Israeli invasion of Lebanon in June 1982, Reagan ordered Israel out of Beirut and deployed 800 US Marines to Lebanon to participate in a multinational peacekeeping operation for a limited period. This decision aimed at establishing a ceasefire in order to prevent a civil war between the

---

© The Author(s), under exclusive license to Springer Nature Switzerland AG 2024
F. Touzani, *Marketing US Foreign Policy in the MENA Region*, Political Campaigning and Communication, https://doi.org/10.1007/978-3-031-45143-0_3

67

Lebanese factions which were supported by Syria and Israel.[1] Additionally, Reagan believed that his decision to send US marines would serve US security interests. He thought that this mission would limit the spread of the Soviet and Syrian influence in Lebanon and the Middle East in general.[2]

However, the continuous human losses in Lebanon, including Americans, prompted 53% of Americans to express their preference for withdrawing US marines from Lebanon in early September 1983.[3] In fact, Reagan was aware of the public disapproval, which was expressed in his diary saying: "On foreign policy, Lebanon, I'm way down. The people just don't know why we're there".[4] Yet, he insisted on keeping US marines despite his awareness of the public disapproval, which he implicitly described as irrational and ignorant saying "The people just don't know why we're there".[5]

The Post-1983 Bombings on US Marines: A Continual Disinterest in Public Opinion

The US Marine barracks were bombarded at Beirut airport on October 23, 1983. The bombings caused more than 200 deaths and more than 100 injuries. Reagan denounced the attacks and described them as the "saddest day of my presidency, perhaps the saddest day of my life".[6] However, Reagan decided to maintain US forces in Lebanon because he believed that their presence served US vital interest in the region despite

---

[1] Ronald Reagan, "Address to the Nation on Lebanon," September 20, 1982. http://millercenter.org/president/reagan/speeches/speech-5453. Accessed January 13, 2020.

[2] Lou Cannon, *President Reagan: The Role of a Lifetime* (New York: Simon & Schuster, 1991), p. 438.

[3] Philip J. Powlick, "Foreign Policy Decisions and Public Opinion: The Case of the Lebanon Intervention, 1982–1984," American Political Science Association (Washington, DC, September 1, 1988), p. 19.

[4] Ronald Reagan, *An American Life* (New York: Simon & Schuster, 1990), p. 447.

[5] Ibid.

[6] Ronald Reagan, "Remarks to Reporters on the Death of American and French Military Personnel in Beirut, Lebanon," October 23, 1983, https://www.reaganlibrary.gov/res earch/speeches/102383a. Accessed November 13, 2019.

3 THE US PUBLIC OPINION: A MARGINAL IMPACT ON US ... 69

Congress's opposition and the remarkable decrease in his public approval rating after the bombings.[7]

As a response to Congress and public disapproval of his decision, Reagan explained his insistence on keeping US forces in Lebanon in an address to the nation four days after the bombings. In this speech, Reagan expressed an unprecedented anti-communist feeling through linking the deadly Beirut attacks to his commitment to block the Soviet expansion in the Middle East.[8] Reagan considered the option of withdrawing the US marines from Lebanon an action of surrendering to terrorists. Reagan said:

> It would say to the terrorists of the world that all it took to change American foreign policy was to murder some Americans and might even cede the region to the Soviet Union.[9]

Despite the fact that Reagan's advisers drew his attention to public increasing disagreement with him and the negative impact this might have on the possibility of being re-elected in the upcoming 1984 presidential elections, Reagan rejected the public opinion and refused to change his policy based on a personal political conviction.[10] By February 1984, the situation has increasingly worsened in Lebanon with the fall of the central government and the disunion of the Lebanese army. As a result, the US marines became more vulnerable to more potential attacks. This prompted some members of Reagan's administration, including Bush, Baker, Weinberger, and McFarlane, to think of a solution that would appeal to Reagan and involve an immediate withdrawal of the marines. Bush suggested withdrawing US marines from Lebanon and continuing US support to the Lebanese central government through naval and air interventions, which Reagan accepted.[11] By February 26, all US forces were withdrawn from Lebanon.

---

[7] Lou Cannon, *President Reagan: The Role of a Lifetime*, pp. 445–449.

[8] Ronald Reagan, "Speech to the nation on Lebanon and Grenada," October 27, 1983, https://www.dakamconferences.org/politsci. Accessed January 21, 2020.

[9] Reagan, *An American Life*, pp. 461–462.

[10] Ronald Reagan, "News Conference of December 20," Department of State Bulletin 84 (1984): 7–8.

[11] Cannon, *Role of a Lifetime*, pp. 454–456.

70 F. TOUZANI

In sum, Reagan's case showed that US public opinion had no impact on his foreign policy decisions pertaining to US military presence in Lebanon. Reagan was mainly relying on what he perceived as US security interests in the region. Therefore, he considerably neglected the public opinion despite his advisers' advice to take it into consideration.

GEORGE H. W. BUSH AND THE GULF WAR (1990–1991): A HALFHEARTED APPEAL TO THE PUBLIC OPINION

On August 2, 1990, Saddam Hussein, invaded Kuwait, Iraq's neighboring oil-producing country. As a response, Bush boycotted all trade with Iraq, froze this country's assets in the US, tried to isolate Iraq diplomatically, and deployed American forces to Saudi Arabia to deter potential Iraqi attacks. There were no public opinion polls on these decisions. However, the editorial opinion supported these decisions and did not advocate for any forceful response to the Iraqi aggression.[12]

At this point, Bush's main concern was the potential impact of the Iraqi aggression on US national security. In fact, he addressed Americans on this issue few days after the Iraqi invasion of Kuwait. In his speech, Bush talked about the significance of Iraqi oil to the US and asked other oil-producing countries to increase their production to mitigate potential impact this problem might have on the global economy.[13]

The emphasis on oil in Bush's speech stemmed from his fear that Saddam Hussein would take control of 20% of world oil reserves if he continued to take control of Kuwait and 40% in case he ventured doing the same with Saudi Arabia. Indeed, Bush clearly expressed this concern saying:

> I worried that Saddam's intentions went far beyond taking over Kuwait. With an attack on Saudi Arabia, he would have gained control over a tremendous amount of the world's oil supply. ... If he was permitted to

---

[12] John Zaller, "Strategic Politicians, Public Opinion and the Gulf Crisis," in W. Lance Bennett and David L. Paletz (Eds.): *Taken by Storm* (Chicago: University of Chicago Press, 1994), p. 252.

[13] George H. W. Bush, Address on Iraq's invasion of Kuwait. August 8,1990, http://millercenter.org/president/bush/speeches/speech-5529. Accessed January 23, 2020.

3 THE US PUBLIC OPINION: A MARGINAL IMPACT ON US ...   71

get away with that, heaven knows where the world would have gone and what forces would have been unleashed.[14]

Taking into consideration the importance of Iraq for US national security, Bush did not eliminate the option of using force if the economic and diplomatic means did not convince Saddam to withdraw from Kuwait despite his awareness of a possible public opinion opposition, which James Baker, the US Secretary of State, reminded him of:

> I know you're aware of the fact that this has all the ingredients that brought down three of the last five Presidents: a hostage crisis, body bags, and a full-fledged economic recession caused by forty-dollar oil.

The President understood it full well. "I know that, Jimmy, I know that", he said. "But we're doing what's right; we're doing what is clearly in the national interest of the United States. Whatever happens, so be it".[15]

It is clear from Bush's response to Baker's reminder that he was prepared for a possible public opinion opposition in case he chose to wage war on Iraq. Bush's statement also shows that he was aware of the negative impact this opposition might have on his presidency like it had had with his predecessors. We can also deduce from Bush's statement that the possibility of using force against Iraq would be prompted by US national interests, which remains a rational factor. This implies that a potential public opinion opposition to using force would be irrational.

By the end of August 1990, the American public opinion was supportive of Bush's policies in the Gulf. These policies revolved around imposing economic sanctions against Iraq, isolating this country using diplomatic means, and deploying US forces to deter a further Iraqi aggression.[16] However, Bush thought that these non-military means would need a long time to take effect, which would negatively influence US national interests, especially pertaining to the price of oil. As a result, he

[14] George Bush, "A Gulf War Exclusive: President Bush Talking with David Frost," Journal Graphics, Transcript 51, 1996, p. 3.

[15] James A. Baker III, *The Politics of Diplomacy: Revolution, War, and Peace*, 1989–1992 (New York: Putnam, 1995), p. 277.

[16] Douglas C. Foyle, *Counting the Public in: Presidents, Public opinion and Foreign Policy* (Columbia University Press, 1999), p. 214.

72   F. TOUZANI

opted for the military option which had to be executed before the end of March 1991 for several factors. These include the difficult weather circumstances in the region starting April as well as the inception of the Holy month of Ramadan for Muslims.

To prepare for this military attack, Bush decided to raise the number of deployed US soldiers in the region to 200 000 by the end of October 1990.[17] The polls conducted in this period showed a clear public concern about Bush's decision, which resulted in a considerable decline in public support for Bush's policies by the end of November.[18] On November 29, the UN Security Council adopted a resolution authorizing the use of all necessary means to expel Iraq from Kuwait after January 15, 1991 if Iraq decided to remain in Kuwait after this date.[19]

The UN resolution made Bush more determined to use force. On November 30, one day after the adoption of the UN resolution, Bush declared the war on Iraq.[20] Being aware of the public concern, Bush announced "to go the extra mile for peace" with Iraq before January 15 through expressing his willingness to meet the Iraqi minister of foreign affairs, Tariq Aziz. Alternatively, he also suggested to send James Baker to meet Saddam Hussein in an attempt to convince the public that he had used all diplomatic means before using coercive ones.[21]

On January 16, four days after Congress's approval of the war, the attacks started with air strikes followed by ground troops about a month later. The war was a success for the US and the international coalition after completing the mission of the Operation Desert Storm. The victory was declared by Bush in a speech in Congress.[22] Interestingly enough,

---

[17] Zaller, "Strategic Politicians," p. 258.

[18] Foyle, *Counting the Public in*, p. 216.

[19] United Nations Security Council Resolution 678, November 29, 1990, https://digitallibrary.un.org/record/102245?ln=en. Accessed February 2, 2020.

[20] "Bush to Iraq: Let's Talk: Invites Envoy to U.S., May Send Baker to Baghdad," November 30, 1990, *Los Angeles Times*, https://www.latimes.com/archives/la-xpm-1990-11-30-mn-5822-story.html. Accessed February 2, 2020.

[21] Bob Woodward, Bob, *The Commanders* (New York: Simon & Schuster, 1991), p. 337.

[22] George H. W. Bush, Address before a joint Session of Congress on the End of the Gulf War, March 6, 1991, http://millercenter.org/president/bush/speeches/speech-3430. Accessed January 23, 2020.

the public approval of Bush promptly and strikingly increased after the crisis. It oscillated between 70 and 89% until the end of August 1991.[23]

All in all, Bush clearly believed that the public opinion was irrational pertaining to waging war on Iraq. He argued that the use of force against Iraq was prompted by US national security. Bush halfheartedly tried to appeal to the public concern when he offered to send James Baker to meet Saddam Hussein and invited the Iraqi minister of foreign affairs to meet him in DC. However, this was done after the huge increase in the US forces deployed to the region and few weeks only before the end of the UN deadline given to Iraq to withdraw from Kuwait.

BILL CLINTON AND IRAQ: A STRONG PUBLIC OPINION SUPPORT

President Clinton inherited the repercussions of the Gulf War which ended with a ceasefire agreement and a UN Security Council Resolution obligating the Iraqi regime to destroy its chemical and biological weapons. The resolution would also require Iraq to facilitate the work of the United Nations Special Commission (UNSCOM) whose mission was to ensure that Iraq complied with its commitment to eliminate its WMDs facilities.[24]

Iraq could not tolerate the effects of the economic sanctions imposed by the UNSC after the Gulf War. As a result, it remobilized more than 60,000 Iraqi troops near the borders with Kuwait in October 1994 in an attempt to display its frustration with the sanctions. Clinton responded by deploying US troops to the region to block a potential Iraqi invasion of Kuwait. Clinton's decision was strongly supported by US public opinion.

To illustrate, about 74% of Americans expressed their approval of sending US troops to deter Saddam Hussein. Besides, Clinton's approval rating increased by 7 points.[25] This strong support can be attributed to Clinton's presentation of Saddam's Iraq as a repressive regime as well

---

[23] John E. Mueller, *Policy and Opinion in the Gulf War* (Chicago: University of Chicago Press, 1994), pp. 180–81, 217–21.

[24] United Nations Security Council Resolution 687, April 3, 1991, https://www.un.org/Depts/unmovic/documents/687.pdf. Accessed February 4, 2020.

[25] "Iraq and Haiti: The Role of Public Opinion in US Foreign Policy," Arab American Institute, October 17, 1994 https://www.aaiusa.org/w101794. Accessed February 5, 2020.

74 F. TOUZANI

as a threat to the international security and US national interests. The discourse focused on highlighting Saddam's human rights violations, his alleged possession of WMDs, and his attempt to control the Kuwaiti oil. Furthermore, Clinton menaced to use force in case Saddam impeded the inspection mission of the UNSCOM. Clinton's menaces were translated into a series of intense air strikes on Iraqi military installations between December 16 and 19, 1998. He justified his move by Saddam's non-cooperative behavior with the UN inspectors.[26]

The American public opinion strongly supported Clinton's decision. 75% supported the attacks on Iraq and 76% showed a "great deal" or "moderate amount" of confidence in Clinton's competence to cope with the crisis.[27] Moreover, 30% only believed that Clinton's decision was taken to deviate people's attention from the proceedings of his impeachment. Indeed, Clinton's impeachment was delayed because of the Iraqi crisis.[28]

George W Bush and the War on Terror: The Rise and the Fall of the Presidential Manipulation of US Public Opinion

9/11 and Fear: An Insidious Presidential Manipulation of the Public Opinion

The Bush campaign to sell the war on terror began right after September 11 attacks which resulted in a great deal of fear and shock among Americans. This campaign focused on heightening this fear through describing the attacks as "acts of war" and the enemy as hidden and omnipresent. Hence, Bush enthusiastically declared his plan to retaliate without specifying the targets.[29]

---

[26] Bill Clinton, "Transcript: President Clinton Explains Iraq Strike," December 16, 1998, https://edition.cnn.com/ALLPOLITICS/stories/1998/12/16/transcripts/clinton.html. Accessed February 4, 2020.

[27] "Poll: US Public Enforces Clinton's Actions on Iraq," *CNN/USA Today/ Gallup Poll*, December 17, 1998, https://edition.cnn.com/ALLPOLITICS/stories/1998/12/17/iraq.poll/. Accessed February 5, 2020.

[28] Ibid.

[29] George Bush, "Remarks by the President in Photo Opportunity with the National Security Team," September 12, 2001, https://georgewbush-whitehouse.archives.gov/news/releases/2001/09/20010912-4.html. Accessed June 4, 2019.

The results of public opinion polls conducted a couple of days after Bush's September 11 speech clearly mirrored Bush's rhetoric. To illustrate, 79% considered the attacks as "acts of war".[30] Furthermore, 75% approved the option of using force to kill the enemy wherever they hide even if the host country might not be connected to 9/11.[31] These polls provided Bush with public support to launch the war on terror which started in Afghanistan followed by Iraq.

The War on Iraq: A Strong Support of US Public Opinion

After the war in Afghanistan, Bush continued to make use of fear to garner continual public support for his war on Iraq. He launched a huge PR campaign which aimed at conveying alarming messages to convince Americans that Saddam's regime possessed WMDs, had strong connections to terrorist groups, and violated human rights.[32]

In fact, Bush's PR campaign, which took advantage of the overwhelming atmosphere of fear in the US, appealed to the majority of Americans in 2002 and early 2003 according to the opinion polls conducted by different polling organizations. These polls showed an increasing support for Bush's war agenda based on the president's pretexts.[33]

---

[30] "CNN/USA Today/Gallup Poll," Polling Report, September 14–15, 2001, http://www.pollingreport.com/terror10.htm. Accessed June 3, 2019.

[31] "NBC News/Wall Street Journal Poll," Polling Report, September 15–16, 2001, http://www.pollingreport.com/terror10.htm. Accessed June 3, 2019.

[32] Bush PR campaign included a series of speeches he delivered in many national and international settings, all of which reiterated these three frames. These include: George Bush, "Presidents Remarks at The United Nations General Assembly", September 12, 2002, https://georgewbush-whitehouse.archives.gov/news/releases/2002/09/20020912-1.html; George Bush, "President Bush outlined Iraqi Threat," October 7, 2002, https://georgewbush-whitehouse.archives.gov/news/releases/2002/10/20021007-8.html; George Bush, "State of the Union Address," January 28, 2003, http://whitehouse.georgewbush.org/news/2003/012803-SOTU.asp. Accessed February 12, 2020.

[33] These include CNN/ USA Today/Gallup Poll, Polling Report, December 9–10, 2002; ABC News/Washington Post Poll, Polling Report, February 6–9, 2003; ABC News Poll, Polling Report, March 5–9, 2003; www.pollingreport.com/iraq18.htm. Accessed February 12, 2020.

The Post-War Era: The Fall of Bush Rhetoric and the Shift in the US Public Opinion

The shift in US public opinion after the war in Iraq can be attributed to many factors. To begin with, no WMDs were found in Iraq, which meant that Americans were deceived by Bush and his administration. To illustrate, most Americans believed that the US made the wrong decision going to war and thought that war was not going well.[34] In addition, the majority of Americans believed that Bush deliberately misled the US on WMDs and the US made a mistake sending in troops.[35]

The change in US public opinion was also prompted by its moral concern about the war. This concern resulted from its awareness of the increasing number of deaths among US troops and Iraqi civilians. More than 60% of Americans surveyed knew that 3000 US forces were killed in Iraq by 2007.[36] Furthermore, the aftermaths of the war discredited Bush's concern for Saddam's human rights abuses before the war, especially after the terrible torture scandal of Abu Ghraib prison and the Guantanamo Bay human rights abuses.

The Abu Ghraib scandal uncovered shocking images of physical, psychological, and sexual abuses as well as horrible killings of Iraqi prisoners by American forces and investigators. This scandal resulted in an increase in public opposition to the war.[37]

The discrediting of Bush's rhetoric about human rights was further emphasized by the US human rights abuses in Guantanamo Bay despite Bush's endeavors to relate the prison's detainees to terrorism. The abuses included urinating on the Koran, tearing its pages out, and abusively commenting on them in addition to torturing the prisoners physically,

[34] Polling Report, "Pew Research Center Survey," Polling Report, April 18–22, 2007, http://www.pollingreport.com/iraq6.htm. Accessed February 21, 2020.

[35] "Iraq," Gallup, 2013, https://news.gallup.com/poll/1633/iraq.aspx. Accessed February 21, 2020.

[36] Anthony R. DiMaggio, *When Media Goes to War: Hegemonic Discourse, Public Opinion, and the Limits of Dissent* (New York: Monthly Review Press, 2009), chap. 7.

[37] Many pollsters associated the sudden decrease in Bush's public approval to Abu Ghraib scandal. See Jeffrey M. Jones and Joseph Carroll, "Deconstructing the Drop in Bush's Public Approval Rating," Gallup, June 1, 2004, https://news.gallup.com/poll/11872/deconstructing-drop-bushs-job-approval-rating.aspx. Accessed February 21, 2020.

3 THE US PUBLIC OPINION: A MARGINAL IMPACT ON US ...   77

psychologically, and sexually.[38] Almost 80% of the prisoners between 2002 and 2013 were freed without any charge.[39] Surprisingly enough, the US Supreme Court refused to denote Guantanamo detainees as "enemy combatants" twice and ordered their civilian trials.[40] These human rights abuses engendered an increasing support for a withdrawal from Iraq.[41]

BARACK OBAMA AND THE ARAB UPRISINGS: A PARTIAL APPEAL TO PUBLIC OPINION

The Arab uprisings of 2010 coincided with Obama's first term. The uprisings' main purpose was to attain democracy and social justice. Some of these uprisings brought about regime change in Tunisia, Egypt, Libya, and Yemen while others engendered political reforms. While most of the uprisings were peaceful, few were armed such as the ones in Libya and Syria.

The American Intervention in Libya: A Skeptical but Supportive Public Opinion

The Libyan armed uprising against Gaddafi's regime began in February 2011. The aggressive suppression of the rebels by Gaddafi's forces resulted in an increase in the number of civilians killed in addition to deteriorating human conditions characterized by a very difficult access to water. These humanitarian conditions were used by Obama, along with

---

[38] "Report Details Alleged Abuse of Guantanamo Bay, Abu Ghraib Detainees," *NewsHour*, PBS, June 18, 2008, https://www.pbs.org/newshour/nation/military-jan-jun e08-detainees_06-18. Accessed February 21, 2020.

[39] Andrew O'Hehir, "Guantanamo: It's Obama's Disgrace Now," *Salon*, May 4, 2013, https://www.salon.com/2013/05/04/guantanamo_its_obamas_disgrace_now/. Accessed February 21, 2020.

[40] Linda Greenhouse, "The Supreme Court: Detainees; Access to Courts," *New York Times*, June 29, 2004, https://www.nytimes.com/2004/06/29/us/the-supreme-court-detainees-access-to-courts.html. Accessed February 21, 2020.

[41] David W. Moore, "Majority of Americans Oppose War With Iraq," *Gallup News Service*, June 21, 2005, https://news.gallup.com/poll/16981/majority-americans-opp ose-war-iraq.aspx. Accessed February 23, 2020.

his concern for establishing democracy in Libya, to justify his militarily intervention in this country.[42]

The intervention managed to kill Gaddafi and the rebels were recognized as the legal representative of Libya by the UN. However, the intervention was denounced by human rights organizations due to the increasing number of civilian deaths. Additionally, the fact that Obama did not express the same concern for democracy with other Arab uprisings made his claim less credible, especially after the long US silence about Gaddafi's repressive regime. The only historic US reaction to Gaddafi was when this latter challenged the US capitalist system and made exploiting Libya's oil hard and pricy for the US and international oil corporations. This implies that one of the major reasons behind Obama's decision to intervene in Libya was this country's oil resources.

The polls conducted before the US intervention showed many reservations about most policy options in Libya, except toppling Gaddafi, which was supported by the majority of Americans.[43] To illustrate, 13% only supported sending US forces; 16% approved attacking Gaddafi's air military facilities while 23% agreed on providing the rebels with military equipment and 44% preferred the option of imposing a no-fly zone.[44] In contrast, when Obama decided to impose a no-fly zone and participate in multinational air strikes on Gaddafi's military facilities, the majority of Americans supported these strikes and approved the way Obama was handling the Libyan crisis.

The public opinion support to Obama's intervention can be attributed to several factors. First, the intervention was an international decision that involved the participation of many countries in addition to the fact that it was approved by the UN Security Council Resolution 1973.[45] Second,

---

[42] Barack Obama, "Remarks by the President on the Middle East and North Africa," May 19, 2011, https://obamawhitehouse.archives.gov/the-press-office/2011/05/19/remarks-president-middle-east-and-north-africa. Accessed February 23, 2020.

[43] CNN/Opinion Research Corporation Poll, Polling Report, March 11–13, 2011; CNN/ Opinion Research Corporation Poll Poll, Polling Report, March 18–20, 2011, https://www.pollingreport.com/libya.htm. Accessed February 24, 2020.

[44] Pew Research Center Poll, *Polling Report*, March 10–13, 2011, https://www.pollingreport.com/libya.htm.
Accessed February 24, 2020.

[45] "United Nations Security Council Resolution 1973," March 17, 2001, https://www.undocs.org/S/RES/1973%20(2011). Accessed February 24, 2020.

3 THE US PUBLIC OPINION: A MARGINAL IMPACT ON US ...   79

US public opinion has generally been supportive of the commander-in-chief in times of war despite the possible skepticism it might show before the war. Third, Obama's framing of the intervention as a humanitarian one appealed to most Americans, which is justified by the fact that the majority supported overthrowing Gaddafi.[46] Obama stated that his decision to intervene aimed to "protect civilians from Gaddafi's attacks".[47]

Obama and the Syrian Crisis: An Unprecedented Public Opinion Impact on the President's War Plans

Being violently suppressed by Assad's regime, the Syrian peaceful uprising developed into a civil war. This war became more complicated with the rise of ISIL. This organization fought against Assad who was supported by Iran and Russia.

Obama's first reactions to the Syrian uprising were reserved, especially with the possibility of a US military intervention. Apart from lamenting the increasing number of deaths among civilians, Obama talked about a "red line" which would potentially prompt him to think about intervening in Syria in case this line is trespassed by Al-Assad. The red line refers to the use of chemical or biological weapons.[48]

Obama took advantage of a UN statement which declared the use of chemical weapons in Syria in September 2013, He promptly started a PR campaign intending to garner public support to use force against Assad's regime.[49] In this campaign, Obama's rhetoric focused on mourning the death of hundreds including women and children to justify the necessity of a US intervention.[50] However, this humanitarian rhetoric was

---

[46] Ibid., 55.

[47] NBC News/Wall Street Journal Poll, Polling Report, March 31–April 4, 2011, https://www.pollingreport.com/libya.htm. Accessed February 24, 2020.

[48] Barack Obama, " Remarks by the President at AIPAC Policy Conference," March 4, 2012 https://obamawhitehouse.archives.gov/the-press-office/2012/03/04/remarks-president-aipac-policy-conference-0 Accessed February 24, 2020.

[49] United Nations, "United Nations Mission to Investigate Allegations of the Use of Chemical Weapons in the Syrian Arab Republic," August 21, 2013, https://www.un.org/zh/focus/northafrica/cwinvestigation.pdf. Accessed February 24, 2020.

[50] Barack Obama, "Remarks of the President in an address to the nation on Syria," September 10, 2013, https://obamawhitehouse.archives.gov/the-press-office/2013/09/10/remarks-president-address-nation-syria. Accessed February 24, 2020.

80   F. TOUZANI

not convincing for the US public opinion taking into consideration that the UN report did not hold Al Assad responsible for the use of chemical weapons. Most Americans refused Obama's attempts to sell a US intervention in Syria and believed that a US military intervention would worsen the conflict.[51]

The strong rejection of Obama's war intention in Syria by the public and Congress prompted him to abandon his interventionist plan and explore an alternative option which focuses on using diplomatic means. The alternative option was an agreement which was managed by the UN and mediated by Russia. The agreement required the Syrian regime to destroy its chemical weapons by mid-2014.[52] The change in Obama's policy plans toward Syria appealed to most Americans as 61% supported the president's agreement with the Syrian government.[53]

This chapter examined the role of the US public opinion in shaping US foreign policy in the MENA region from Ronald Reagan's presidency to Barack Obama's. We analyzed the presidents' policies with a focus on the US military interventions as well as the results of public opinion polls about relevant issues. The chapter aimed at evaluating the US public opinion's degree of influence on the Presidents' decisions to use force.

Generally speaking, the analyses revealed that the US public opinion is rarely influential when it comes to using force in the region, especially pertaining to the use of force in the Middle East and North Africa. The limited role of the public opinion in the US stems from two main factor. First, The presidents may ignore Americans's opinion thinking that they are not rational, especially pertaining to their understanding of US national interests. Second, Americans can be manipulated by the presidential discourse through PR campaigns. These campaigns strive to frame particular problems in a specific manner to win the public support. In

---

[51] "Public Opinion Runs Against Syrian Air Strikes," Pew Research Center, September 3, 2013, https://www.pewresearch.org/wp-content/uploads/sites/4/legacy-pdf/9-3-13-Syria-Release.pdf. Accessed February 24, 2020.

[52] "UN Security Council Agrees to Rid Syria of Chemical Weapons, Endorses Peace Process," *UN News*, September 27, 2013, https://news.un.org/en/story/2013/09/451502-un-security-council-agrees-rid-syria-chemical-weapons-endorses-peace-process. Accessed February 24, 2020.

[53] Polling Report, "CNN/ORC Poll," September 10, 2013, http://www.pollingreport.com/syria2.htm. Accessed February 24, 2020.

short, if the US public opinion does not agree with the presidents' foreign policy thoughts, they can either ignore or manipulate it.

The following chapter deals with the role of another non-state actor in shaping US foreign policy decisions in the region. That is to say, interest groups. In fact, a significant work of interest groups revolves around targeting the public opinion to win its voice and use it or mobilize it to put pressure on decision makers.

CHAPTER 4

Interest Groups: An Imperfect Impact

INTEREST GROUPS: DEFINITIONS AND CLASSIFICATION

Interest Groups: A Broadly Defined Concept

Humans have historically developed a natural and solid leaning toward clustering together to achieve shared goals. Such objectives include but not limited to defending their rights, advocating for particular causes, or attaining economic benefits. Interest groups, also referred to as lobbies or pressure groups, are difficult to define due to the fact that their work is so varied and their interests are often very broad. The fact that there are numerous definitions for interest groups indicates that there has been no scholarly unanimity around a distinct definition, especially among political scientists. Thus, interest groups are often broadly defined.

Most definitions indicate that interest groups are a formal association of individuals or organizations that share similar goals and concerns and aim at influencing policies through lobbying.[1] David Truman defined interest groups as "any group that, on the basis of one or more shared attitudes, makes certain claims upon other groups in society".[2] Similarly, Almond

---

[1] Laura Baroni, Brendan Carroll and Adam William Chalmers et al., "Defining and Classifying Interest Groups," Interest Groups & Advocacy 3 (2014): 149–151.

[2] David Truman, *The Governmental Process Political Interests and Public Opinion* (New York: Alfred A. Knopf, 1951), p. 33.

© The Author(s), under exclusive license to Springer Nature Switzerland AG 2024
F. Touzani, *Marketing US Foreign Policy in the MENA Region*, Political Campaigning and Communication,
https://doi.org/10.1007/978-3-031-45143-0_4

and Powell defined interest groups as "group of individuals who are linked by a particular bond or concern of advantage and who have awareness of those bonds".[3] According to Hitchner and Levine, an interest group is "a collection of individuals who try to realize their common objectives by influencing public policy",[4] In a relatively more recent literature, Grant's definition focuses on the importance of interest groups in influencing the establishment and implementation of policies.[5]

These definitions share two major characteristics about interest groups. First, they constitute of individuals who share the same or similar values and goals. Second, they seek to influence policies through exerting pressure on policymakers. This chapter answers the following questions: Why interest groups succeed or fail to shape US foreign policy in the Middle East and North Africa? Under which circumstances and using which strategies might interest groups influence foreign policy making in the region?

Interest Groups: A Variously Categorized Concept

The fact that interest groups have various interests and goals explains the various scholarly classification schemes used to categorize these entities.[6]

The most important classification of interest groups was provided by Almond, Powell et al. who classified interest groups in four categories.[7] The first category is the anomic groups. These groups are informally and spontaneously established with no prior coordination or organization by its members. The anomic groups' members usually share the same strong feeling about a particular issue, which often prompts them to express

---

[3] Gabriel A. Almond and G. Bingham Powell, Jr., *Comparative Politics Today: A World View* (Boston, 1980), p. 35.

[4] Dell Hitchner and Carole Levine, *Comparative Government and Politics* (New York, Dodd Mead & Co. 1967), p. 59.

[5] Wyn Grant, *Pressure Groups and British Politics* (London: MacMillan Press Ltd, 2002), p. 14.

[6] In addition to Almond's classification, Jean Blondel and Maurice Duverger provided two other classifications that, in their essence, follow a similar pattern to that of Almond's. See Blondel's, *Comparative Government a Reader. Garden City* (NY: Anchor Books, 1969) and Duverger's, *Party Politics and Pressure Groups* (Thomas Nelson & Sons Ltd, 1972).

[7] Gabriel Aiomnd, Bingham Powell, Aare Strom and R. J. Dalton, *Comparative Politics Today: A World View*, (Singapore: Pearson Education, Inc, 2000), pp. 70–72.

it concurrently through street demonstrations or violent actions in an attempt to influence policies in an unconventional manner.

The second category is the non-associational groups which are also more likely to be disorganized and irregular in their lobbying endeavors. However, their work tend to be more persistent than anomic groups because their concerns revolve around ethnic, regional, religions, or occupational problems.

The third category is the institutional groups which are formally and highly organized. These groups might play various social or political roles in addition to interest articulations. As a result, their work is often very impactful. Examples include factions within political parties, Congressional entities, administrative groups, armies, churches, or corporations. This category's interests are often restricted to the group they represent.

The fourth category is the associational groups which are formally organized to represent the interests of specific groups whose main purpose revolves around economic benefits. Hence, such groups often aim at influencing policies.

These four categories can be re-classified in two major ones each of which constitutes of few sub-categories.

The first major category is economic/business interest groups whose major concern is to defend the economic interests and benefits of their members. These include corporations, trade unions, and institutional associations representing some key sectors such as education and health.

The second major category is the citizens interest groups whose purpose revolves around non-vocational goals. These include identity groups which assemble citizens with similar ideological, ethnic, and religious interests in addition to public interest groups with specific concerns including environmental and humanitarian organizations.

Case Selection, Data Collection, and Methodology
Taking into consideration that this chapter examines the role of interest groups in shaping US foreign policy in the Middle East and North Africa, the choice of interest group should be relevant to the major strategic US interests in the region. These interests have been historically and constantly pursued by US policymakers since the end of the Second World

War. That is to say, protecting Israel and maintaining the flow of oil.[8] This is in addition to relatively recent interests such as fighting terrorism and hindering the development of nuclear weapons.

There are many US ethnic, religious, business, and civil interest groups whose agenda relates to US strategic interests in the region. The most important among those are: The American Israel Public Affairs Committee (AIPAC), Christians United for Israel (CUFI), the National Association of Arab Americans (NAAA), the Council on American Islamic Relations (CAIR), ExxonMobil, and the Center for Arms Control and Non-Proliferation.

It is important to point out that the scope of this chapter does not allow examining the role of all of those interest groups in shaping US foreign policy in the MENA region. Therefore, we chose the American Israel Public Affairs Committee (AIPAC) because it is the largest and the most powerful US interest group whose agenda focuses on major issues relating to US strategic interest in the region.

Fortune magazine carried out a survey to ask members of Congress and their staff about their opinion on the most powerful interest groups in the US. The results of the survey revealed that AIPAC ranked second after the American Association of Retired Persons (AARP).[9] The same finding was reached by the National Journal in another study.[10]

Taking into account that this research was conducted from Morocco, it was very difficult to conduct interviews, especially with representatives of AIPAC as well as members of Congress or congressional staffers. Consequently, we mainly relied on qualitative analysis of data published by the media, AIPAC, and the government. These include but not limited to articles, speeches, reports, and congressional official documents such as bills and resolutions.

[8] Daniel Byman and Sara Bjerg Miller, "Thé United States and the Middle East: Interest, Risks and Risks," *Sustainable Security*, 2016, p. 263. 10.1093/acprof:oso/978 0190611477.003.0011.

[9] Jefferey H. Birnbaum, "Washington's Poser 25," *Fortune*, December 8, 1997.

[10] Richard E. Cohen and Peter Bell, "Congressional Insiders Poll," National Journal, March 5, 2005.

4 INTEREST GROUPS: AN IMPERFECT IMPACT

AMERICAN ISRAEL PUBLIC AFFAIRS COMMITTEE (AIPAC)

AIPAC's main mission is to "strengthen, protect and promote the US-Israel relationship in ways that enhance the security of the United States and Israel".[11] To achieve this mission, AIPAC tries to gain access to policymakers and influence their decisions through the use of an effective combination of various strategies. These strategies include lobbying Congress and the executive, providing financial campaign contributions to legislative candidates in addition to shaping the public opinion through monitoring and influencing the media, academia and foreign policy think tanks.[12]

To find out why AIPAC succeeds or fails to shape US foreign policy in the Middle East and North Africa, under which circumstances and using which strategies, we focused on the presidencies of George W. Bush and Barack Obama in the light of two important issues pertaining to US foreign policy in the MENA area and AIPAC's agenda. That is to say, the Arab-Israeli conflict and the Iran nuclear program.

We will start with highlighting AIPAC's lobbying strategies followed by discussing how AIPAC gains access to policymakers before examining whether this interest group was successful in influencing US foreign policy pertaining to the Arab-Israeli Conflict and Iran nuclear program during the presidencies of George W. Bush and Barack Obama.

AIPAC's Lobbying Strategies: A Multivariate Grass-root Approach to Shaping and Dominating the US Public Opinion

AIPAC strives to persuade Americans that US and Israel's values are not distinct and their strategic interests in the Middle East are identical. To do so, it often plays the anti-Semitism card and presents a partial viewpoint about Israel's policies in the region. Moreover, AIPAC makes considerable efforts to silence criticism of Israel's policies or mark down the voices which highlight the identicalness of US and Israel's interests.[13] This is carried out through various means such as the media, academia, and think tanks because of their crucial role in shaping the public opinion.

---

[11] AIPAC website homepage, https://www.aipac.org. Accessed March 30, 2020.

[12] John J. Mearsheimer and Stephen M. Walt, *The Israel' Lobby and US Foreign Policy* (Farrar, Straus, and Giroux, 2007), pp. 151–167.

[13] Ibid.

Monitoring and Influencing the Media: An Effective Tactic to Shape the Public Opinion

While it is obsolete to argue that AIPAC or the Jews control what the US media say about Israel, it is safe to say that the Israel lobby, especially AIPAC, manages to influence the media through hard work and perseverance. A recent and very large media study conducted by 416Labs, a Toronto-based research group, on the headlines of five impactful US newspapers from 1967 to 2017 revealed a continuous pro-Israel bias coverage of the Israel-Palestine conflict.[14] One would ask what are the sources of this biased coverage?

First, such a bias implies that AIPAC takes advantage of a significant number of pro-Israel journalists and reporters in US mainstream media and the relatively rare media professionals who are pro-Arab. Eric Alterman, an American journalist, historian, and a media critic, provided a list of 56 "columnists and commentators who can be counted upon to support Israel reflexively and without qualification".[15] In contrast, he counted only 5 media professionals who persistently criticize Israel's policies or support pro-Arab ones.[16]

Second, AIPAC makes use of various tactics to block and limit unsympathetic news on Israel. These include mobilizing people to send mass messages to editors and media executives, organize protests and boycott the news outlets which present disadvantageous comments on Israel. Eason Jordan, the CNN chief news manager, reported that he once received about 6000 e-mail messages in one day denouncing a perceived

---

[14] The newspapers on which the study was conducted are the *Chicago Tribune, Los Angeles Times, New York Times, Washington Post*, and *Wall Street Journal*. For more information on the study see 416 Labs, "50 years of occupation," December 19, 2018, https://static1.squarespace.com/static/558067a3e4b0cb2f81614c38/t/5c391c c4758d46ef9834907f/1547246789711/416_LABS_50_Years_Of_Occupation_Jan+9th. pdf. Accessed March 31, 2020.

[15] Eric Alterman, "Intractable Foes, Warring Narratives," MSNBC.com, March 28, 2002, https://www.wrmea.org/002-may/intractable-foes-warring-narratives-measur ing-the-unmeasurable.html. Accessed April 1, 2020.

[16] Ibid. Despite the minor challenges that Alterman's argument encountered, the gap between pro-Israel commentators and those criticizing it is too large to weaken the essence of Alterman's argument.

4 INTEREST GROUPS: AN IMPERFECT IMPACT   89

anti-Israel comments by a CNN correspondent in Jerusalem.[17] Furthermore, the major mainstream US newspapers have been boycotted at some point as a result of their reporting on Israel's policies in the Middle East including the New York Times, the Washington Post, the Los Angeles Times, the Chicago Tribune, the Miami Herald, and the Philadelphia Inquirer.[18]

The strength of AIPAC's pressure makes some journalists think twice before criticizing Israel. This is confirmed by a corespondent of a large US newspaper as quoted by Michael Massing saying that newspapers are "afraid" of organizations such as AIPAC: "The pressure from these groups is relentless. Editors would just as soon not touch them".[19] Similarly, Menachem Shalev, the former spokesperson of Israel's consulate in New York, stated:

> Of course, a lot of self-censorship goes on. Journalists, editors, and politicians are going to think twice about criticizing Israel if they know they are going to get thousands of angry calls in a matter of hours. The Jewish lobby is good at orchestrating pressure.[20]

Winning the War of Ideas: Toward Controlling the World of Think Tanks in Washington

Being aware of the fact that the US news media are increasingly relying on think tanks for policy analysis as well as these latter's key role in providing legislators and executives with policy ideas, AIPAC was convinced of the necessity to establish pro-Israel think tanks that aim at shaping US foreign policy in the Middle East in favor of Israel.

---

[17] Felicity Barringer, "Mideast Turmoil: The News Outlets; Some U.S. Backers of Israel Boycott Dailies Over Mideast Coverage That They Deplore," *New York Times*, May 23, 2002, https://www.nytimes.com/2002/05/23/world/mideast-turmoil-outlets-some-us-backers-israel-boycott-dailies-over-mideast.html. Accessed April 1, 2020.

[18] David Shaw, "From Jewish Outlook, Media Are Another Enemy," *Los Angeles Times*, April 28, 2002, https://www.latimes.com/archives/la-xpm-2002-apr-28-mn-40500-story.html and Michael Massing, "The Storm Over the Israel Lobby," *New York Review of Books*, June 8, 2006, https://www.nybooks.com/articles/2006/06/08/the-storm-over-the-israel-lobby/. Accessed April 1, 2020.

[19] Michael Massing, "The Israel Lobby", *The Nation*, May 23, 2002, https://www.thenation.com/article/archive/israel-lobby/. Accessed April 1, 2020.

[20] David Biale, *Power and Powerlessness in Jewish History* (NewYork: Schocken Books, 1986), 186–187.

90 F. TOUZANI

The Washington Institute for Near East Policy (WINEP) or the Washington Institute is one of those think tanks which were funded by AIPAC's donors and established by former AIPAC officials. These include Barbi Weinberg, AIPAC's former vice president and the wife of Larry Weinberg, AIPAC's former president in addition to Martin Indyk, AIPAC's former deputy director for research and a former US ambassador to Israel.[21]

The institute identifies itself as "the largest research institute devoted exclusively to the study of the the Middle East".[22] Its board of directors include Shelly Kassen, James Schreiber, Bernard Leventhal, Peter Lowy, Walter P. Stern, Jay Bernstein, Moses S. Libitzky, and Lief D. Rosenblatt. They are all known for defending US foreign policies that serve, first and foremost, Israel's interests.[23] In addition to the Washington Institute, the pro-Israel lobby has maintained an influential presence in other prominent think tanks in Washington. Most of these think tanks are pro-Israel and hardly criticize US absolute support for Israel.[24]

Martin Indyk, AIPAC's former deputy director for research and one of the founders of the Washington Institute, was the founding director of the Saban Center for Middle East Policy, a research institute affiliated with the Brookings Institution. The institutions ranked on top of all think tanks in the world in several years since 2008 including the 2019 report.[25] The Saban Center was initially funded by a generous contribution of $13 million from Haim Saban, a staunch Zionist who was depicted by the New York Times as "perhaps the most politically connected mogul in Hollywood, throwing his weight and money around Washington and, increasingly, the world, trying to influence all things Israeli".[26]

---

[21] Thomas G. Mitchell, *Israel /Palestine and the Politics of a Two-State Future* (McFarland, 2013), p. 164.

[22] The Washington Institute for Near East Studies, Mission and History, https://www.washingtoninstitute.org/about/mission-and-history. Accessed April 2, 2020.

[23] The Washington Institute for Near East Studies, Board of Directors. https://www.washingtoninstitute.org/about/board-of-directors. Accessed April 2, 2020.

[24] Mearsheimer and Walt, 2007, pp. 176–177.

[25] James G. McGann, TTCSP Global Go To Think Tank Index Report, *University of Pennsylvania*, https://repository.upenn.edu/think_tanks/. Accessed April 2, 2020.

[26] Andrew Ross Sorkin, "Schlepping to Moguldom," *New York Times*, September 5, 2004. https://www.nytimes.com/2004/09/05/business/yourmoney/schlepping-to-mog uldom.html, Accessed April 2, 2020.

4 INTEREST GROUPS: AN IMPERFECT IMPACT   91

Keeping an Eye on Academia: A Less Effective Tactic
The failure of Oslo accords and Ariel Sharon's use of deplorable force against the Palestinians in 2002 during the Second Intifada prompted a widespread criticism of Israel in US campuses. As a response, AIPAC intensified its endeavors to reshape the students' opinion about Israel through multiplying the funds allocated for college programs that aimed at preparing college students to endorse Israel's position.

In 2003, AIPAC assembled a group of 240 students leaders from different US campuses to participate in a four-day fully funded training in Washington. The training's main purpose was to teach these students how to regain their peers' hearts and minds in favor of Israel's policies in the occupied territories.[27] Four years later, a larger assembly was organized by AIPAC during its annual Policy Conference which hosted about 400 US campuses represented by 1200 college students including 150 presidents of student governments.[28]

AIPAC's website dedicates an entire section titled "AIPAC on Campus". The section provides information on AIPAC's campus initiatives in US colleges and universities as well as training and internship opportunities at the organization.[29]

These attempts to influence students went hand in hand with a similar campaign to monitor and put pressure on faculty members who exhibited a certain kind of criticism to Israel. This process started with the identification of the faculty and campus entities that are suspect of being anti-Israel. The results of this survey were released in the 1984 AIPAC College Guide: Exposing the Anti-Israel Campaign on Campus.[30] Tracking critics of Israel in the academia was further developed in 2002 through the establishment of Campus Watch, a website that incited students to report professors who might show or express an anti-Israel attitude. This website

---

[27] James D. Besser, "Turning Up Heat in Campus Wars," *Jewish Week*, July 25, 2003.

[28] Northern Nazarene University, *Messenger* 95 (2) (Summer): 2007, https://web.nnu.edu/files/alumni/summer_07.pdf. Accessed April 3, 2020.

[29] AIPAC on Campus, https://www.aipac.org/connect/students. Accessed April 6, 2020.

[30] Jonathan S. Kessler and Jeff Schwaber, *The AIPAC college Guide: Exposing the Anti-Israel Campaign on Campus, AIPAC papers on U.S.-Israel Relations* (American Israel Public Affairs Committee, 1984).

92 F. TOUZANI

was criticized for threatening the blacklisted professors and infringe on their intellectual freedom.[31]

The pressure has also been put on the administrators of prominent universities which hire some prominent professors, especially those who are thought to be critical of Israel. Examples of this pressure include the hundreds of e-mail messages and phone calls that Jonathan Cole, the former provost at Columbia University, received after recruiting Rashid Khalidi, the prominent Palestinian-American historian. The same thing happened with the late literary critic Edward Said when he expressed his opinion about Israel's policies in the occupied territories.[32]

Furthermore, to foster pro-Israel discourse in academia and apart from the numerous existing Jewish studies programs, some AIPAC philanthropists have funded new academic programs focusing on Israel in many US institutions of higher education. These programs would contribute in minimizing anti-Israel rhetoric and further spread the pro-Israel discourse in US colleges and universities.[33] According to an Association of Jewish Studies' 2018 survey, there were 250 Jewish Studies programs in American colleges and universities.[34] Additionally, there are about 27 programs of Israel Studies in prominent American Universities.[35]

[31] Michael Massing, "Campus Watch," *The New York Review of Books*, July 13, 2006, https://www.nybooks.com/articles/2006/07/13/campus-watch/; Kristine McNeil, "The War on Academic Freedom," *The Nation*, November 11, 2002, https://www.thenation.com/article/archive/war-academic-freedom/. Accessed April 3, 2020.

[32] Jonathan R. Cole, "The Patriot Act on Campus: Defending the University Post-9/11," *Boston Review*, Summer 2003, http://bostonreview.net/us/jonathan-r-cole-patriot-act-campus. Accessed April 3, 2020.

[33] Mitchell G. Bard, "Tenured or Tenuous: Defining the Role of Faculty in Supporting Israel on Campus," *The Israel on Campus Coalition and the American-Israeli Cooperative Enterprise*, May 2004.

[34] Ilana Horwitz, Arielle Levites and Emily Sigalow, "Jewish Studies in the Academy in 2018," Association for Jewish Studies, https://www.associationforjewishstudies.org/docs/default-source/surveys-of-the-profession/final-report_infographic_7-29-2.pdf?sfvrsn=2. Accessed April 3, 2020.

[35] "Israel Education: University Centers of Israel Studies," Jewish Virtual Library, https://www.jewishvirtuallibrary.org/university-chairs-in-israel-studies-2. Accessed April 3, 2020.

4 INTEREST GROUPS: AN IMPERFECT IMPACT   93

Targeting Specific Communities: A Direct Contact with Americans
AIPAC's website dedicates an entire section titled "communities". This section details AIPAC's efforts and initiatives to advocate for its pro-Israel agenda among US religious, ethnic, business, and professional communities. These include AIPAC's Synagogue Initiative, the Christian community, the African American community, the Hispanic community, the Real Estate Business, and Los Angelos Legal community.[36]

Gaining Access to Policymakers: Various Means, But One End

Gaining Access to Members of Congress: A Multifaceted Strategy
Money, AIPAC, and Congress: Gaining Access to Future and Current Legislators
First of all, it is important to point out that AIPAC cannot contribute to campaigns of Congressional candidates. However, their individual members can. Taking into consideration that money matters a lot in US legislative elections, AIPAC's strength in generating financial contributions to Congressional candidates allows the organization to gain access to US legislators through rewarding those who endorse favorable US policies to Israel and punish those who do not.[37] The process is carried out through various channels.

Initially, AIPAC's donors are usually key contributors to Congressional candidates. For example, the total contributions of AIPAC's members in 2019 was nearly $3 million.[38] Additionally, AIPAC plays an important role in identifying pro-Israel Congressional candidates and linking them to other contributors and potential funders including pro-Israel Political

---

[36] AIPAC, Communities. https://www.aipac.org/connect/communities. Accessed April 6, 2020.

[37] M. J. Rosenberg, "This Is How AIPAC Really Works," *The Nation*, February 14, 2019, https://www.thenation.com/article/archive/aipac-omar-israel-congress-anti-semitism/. Accessed April 4, 2020.

[38] The exact amount was $2,962,107. This information was based on the data released by the Federal Election Committee (FEC) on March 23, 2020. Center of Responsive Politics, "Pro-Israel contributions summary: 2019–2020," https://www.opensecrets.org/industries/indus.php?cycle=2020&ind=q05. Accessed April 4, 2020.

94   F. TOUZANI

Action Committees (PACs).[39] This is done through overseeing congressional voting records, meeting with all candidates to brief them on Israel's challenges in the Middle East and ask them to write a position paper on how they see the US-Israel relation in order to decide whom the organization would recommend for campaign funding.[40]

The Center for Responsive Politics (CRP), an independent research institute which specializes in tracking campaign donations, counts about 20 pro-Israel PACs. The most powerful campaign donator is J-Street which contributed $1,487,976 during the 2020 election cycle.[41] According to the same center, the total contributions from pro-Israel individuals and PACs from 1990 to 2020 is $151,391,977.[42] However, the use of money to help Israel-friendly congressional candidates get elected is not always successful despite its overall effectiveness.[43]

Reaching-out to Legislators: A Direct Approach to Gain Access
In addition to financial contributions, AIPAC gains access to members of Congress through various direct pro-active means. To begin with, AIPAC is keen on meeting with every single candidate or contact the members' staffers and offer policy advice on issues pertaining to the Middle East in general or Israel in particular. In his speech during the AIPAC policy conference of 2007, Howard Friedman, one of the former AIPAC presidents, emphasizes the importance of meeting with members of Congress and candidates more frequently:

> Each one in this room must make the commitment to meet with our members of Congress and candidates for congressional offices at least twice more after Tuesday's lobbying appointments and before the next policy conference. We can be sure that debates taking place in Congress

[39] David Biale, *Power and Powerlessness in Jewish History* (NewYork: Schocken Books, 1986), pp. 186–187.

[40] IBP USA, *Israel Lobby in the United States Handbook: Volume 1 Strategic Information, Organization, Operations, Performance* (USA International Business Publications, 2018), pp. 14–15.

[41] Center of Responsive Politics. "Pro-Israel Contributors: 2019–2020," https://www.opensecrets.org/industries/contrib.php?cycle=2020&ind=q05. Accessed April 4, 2020.

[42] Center of Responsive Politics, "Pro-Israel Contributions Totals: 1990–2020," https://www.opensecrets.org/industries/totals.php?cycle=2020&ind=q05. Accessed April 4, 2020.

[43] Mearsheimer and Walt, *The Israel Lobby*, pp. 155–169.

4 INTEREST GROUPS: AN IMPERFECT IMPACT 95

will color the views of presidential candidates. Therefore, our Capitol Hill meetings carry more weight than usual. Providing a member of Congress or presidential candidate with AIPAC's reliable information is key.[44]

If AIPAC staffers have to meet all members of Congress at least twice a year, this totals to more than a 1000 meeting annually. Howard explains how they proceed with each meeting saying:

AIPAC meets with every candidate running for Congress. These candidates receive in-depth briefings to help them completely understand the complexities of Israel's predicament and that of the Middle East as a whole. We even ask each candidate to author a 'position paper' on their views of the U.S.-Israel relationship—so it's clear where they stand on the subject.[45]

Second, AIPAC organizes regular briefings on the Capitol Hill for Congressional staffers. It also sends a copy of its monthly policy journal, Near East Report, and AIPAC Briefing Book to all members of Congress to provide "insight and analysis into the issues affecting the U.S.-Israel relationship".[46]

Third, according to one of AIPAC's staffers, AIPAC staffers are usually asked to "draft speeches, work on legislation, advise on tactics, perform research, collect co-sponsors and marshal votes".[47]

Furthermore, the American Israel Education Foundation (AIEF), a pro-Israel charitable organization affiliated with AIPAC, organizes fully funded journeys to Israel for members of Congress accompanied by a member of their families and their staffers to "help educate political leaders and influentials about the importance of the U.S.-Israel relationship through firsthand experiences in Israel, briefings by experts on Middle East affairs, and meetings with Israeli political elite".[48] In the past

---

[44] Howard Friedman, "AIPAC Policy Conference Speech," March 11, 2007, https://www.aipac.org/-/media/publications/policy-and-politics/speeches-and-interviews/spe eches-by-aipac-leadership/2007/03/friedman_pc_2007.pdf. Accessed April 6, 2020.

[45] Ibid., 52.

[46] AIPAC, *Near East Report*, https://www.aipac.org/resources/aipac-publications/. Accessed April 6, 2020.

[47] This is quoted in Camille Mansour, *Beyond Alliance: Israel in U.S. Foreign Policy*, translated by James A.
Cohen (NewYork: Columbia University Press, 1994), p. 242.

[48] American Israel Education Foundation, *Mission Statement*, http://www.aiefdn.org. Accessed April 6, 2020.

decade, AIEF has spent nearly $13 million on journeys for 363 legislators and 657 congressional staffers to Israel.[49]

Inciting Americans to Take Action: An Indirect Approach to Gain Access

AIPAC makes considerable efforts to urge Americans, especially their members to contact their representatives and ask them to support policies that serve Israel's interests and oppose those which do not. AIPAC's Action Center, which can be accessed through its website, provides information about the issues under consideration by Congress as well as how to contact their representatives.[50]

The Legislators' Presence in AIPAC's Events: A Strong Engagement

AIPAC organizes various events to which members of Congress and their staffers are invited to attend and participate in. The largest event is its annual Policy Conference which is often attended by more than two thirds of Congress.[51] In fact, the AIPAC Policy Conference is the largest assembly of members of Congress in one place, excluding the State of the Union Addresses and the joint sessions of Congress.[52]

Gaining Access to Presidents and Presidential Candidates: Money, Turnout, and Personnel

The Presidential Election Campaign: The Power of Jewish Constituency

Despite the fact that Jewish Americans constitute only 2.2% of the total US adult population, their impact on the presidential elections partially

---

[49] Akela Lacy and Ryan Grim, "An Invitation You Can't Refuse: How Rep. Steny Hoyer Makes Sure AIPAC's Israel Junket Is Well Attended," *The Intercept*, June 20, 2019, https://theintercept.com/2019/06/20/steny-hoyer-aipac-j-street-israel/. Accessed April 6, 2020.

[50] AIPAC, Action Center: Contact Congress, https://takeaction.aipac.org/y1wjJP1. Accessed April 6, 2020.

[51] AIPAC Policy Conference 2020, https://event.aipac.org/policyconference-about. Accessed April 6, 2020.

[52] Connie Bruck, "Friends of Israel," *The New Yorker*, August 25, 2014, https://www.newyorker.com/magazine/2014/09/01/friends-israel. Accessed April 6, 2020.

4 INTEREST GROUPS: AN IMPERFECT IMPACT   97

stems from their generous campaign contributions.[53] For instance, about 60% of the funds raised from nonpublic sources come from the pro-Israel lobby which plays a key role in mobilizing Jewish voters to donate.[54]

AIPAC also mobilizes the Jewish constituency to vote for the presidential candidate who is likely to endorse Israel's policies. The Jewish constituency has the highest turnout rates among ethnic constituencies in the US in addition to the fact that it is amassed in decisive states in US elections such as Pennsylvania, California, New York, New Jersey, Illinois, and Florida.[55]

Maintaining the Executive Support: A Staff-Based Means

In order to gain and maintain access to the executive branch, AIPAC is very keen on ensuring that its followers hold control of key positions in the administration. To illustrate, President Clinton relied on many pro-Israel officials to advise on Middle East issues. The most prominent among those were Martin Indyk, the former AIPAC's deputy director of research and one of the founders of WINEB, a pro-Israel think tank. Indyk occupied key positions during Clinton's administration including the assistant Secretary of State, the US ambassador to Israel, and a member of Clinton's National Security Council. Additionally, there was Dennis Ross, a Jew who joined WINEB after serving as Clinton's special delegate to the Middle East.

The Bush administration constituted of more neoconservative pro-Israel and Jewish highly ranked officials with positions related to US policies in the Middle East. The pro-Israel officials who were born to Jewish families included Paul Wolfowitz, Elliot Abrams, Douglas Feith, Scooter (Lewis) Libby, and Richard Perle.[56] As for those who were

[53] Pew Research Center, A Portrait of Jewish Americans: Population Estimates 2013, October 1, 2013, https://www.pewforum.org/2013/10/01/chapter-1-population-estimates/. Accessed April 7, 2020.

[54] Thomas B. Edsall and Alan Cooperman, "GOP Uses Remarks to Court Jews," *The Washington Post*, March 13, 2003, https://www.washingtonpost.com/archive/politics/2003/03/13/gop-uses-remarks-to-court-jews/74571902-fe63-4543-a972-a5d642546321/. Accessed April 7, 2020.

[55] Robert Gregg, Gary W. McDonogh, and Cindy H. Wong, *Encyclopedia of Contemporary American Culture* (Routledge, 2005), p. 390.

[56] Jews in Barack Obama Administration. *Jewish Virtual Library, 2001–2009*, https://www.jewishvirtuallibrary.org/jews-in-the-george-w-bush-administration. Accessed April 8, 2020.

98   F. TOUZANI

not Jewish, but has always exhibited a strong support to Israel, we can mention Dick Cheney, Donald Rumsfeld, John Bolton, Aaron Friedberg, William Luti, David Wurmser, and John Hannah.

Obama's Administration was also peopled by pro-Israel high officials who were born to Jewish families and whose positions were relevant to the Middle East. These included Tony Blinken, Eric Lynn, David Plouffe, Daniel Rubenstein, Steven Simon, Rahm Emanuel, David Axelrod, James Steinberg, Mara Rudman.[57]

The same thing applies to Trump Administration whose pro-Israel Jewish officials working on Middle-East-related issues included Avi Berkowitz, Jared Kushner, David Friedman, Jason Greenblatt, Stephen Miller, and Elan Carr.[58] This is in addition to Mike Pompeo, former US Secretary of State, and John Bolton, former National Security Advisor. They are both well-known for being hawkish pro-Israel advocates.

AIPAC's Policy Conference: The Significant Presence of Presidents and Presidential Candidates

AIPAC has always·been keen on inviting presidents and presidential candidates to deliver speeches at its annual policy conference in order to make their pro-Israel cases. Examples of these speeches include President Bill Clinton (1995 and 1996), presidential candidate George Bush (2000), President Bush (2002), presidential candidate Barack Obama (2008), President Obama (2011 and 2012), Presidential candidate Hillary Clinton (2016), Presidential candidate Donald Trump (2016), Trump's Vice President Pence (2019), and presidential candidate Mike Bloomberg (2020).

---

[57] Jews in Barack Obama Administration, *Jewish Virtual Library, 2009–2017*, https://www.jewishvirtuallibrary.org/jews-in-the-barack-obama-administration. Accessed April 8, 2020.

[58] Jews in Trump Administration, *Jewish Virtual Library, 2017–2020*, https://www.jewishvirtuallibrary.org/jews-in-donald-trump-administration. Accessed April 8, 2020.

AIPAC and US Foreign Policy in the MENA Area: An Imperfect Influence

To examine the effectiveness of AIPAC's lobbying strategies in gaining access to policy makers, we chose some case studies that relate to the organization's agenda and its achievements as highlighted in its website. In so saying, we identified two major policy axes.

First, AIPAC's endeavors to ensure the continuous provision of US aid to strengthen Israel's military might remains one of the primary goals. Second, the organization makes sure to direct US resources to protect Israel's security through supporting its position against the Palestinians and other perceived hostile regimes or movements in the region. This includes preventing those entities from developing Weapons of Mass Destruction (WMDs) and fighting emerging terrorist groups.

The September 11 events have contributed in advancing AIPAC's agenda as the US was turning toward concentrating its foreign policy plans on the Middle East. The focus was on the war on terror, which aimed at toppling Saddam's regime in Iraq for its alleged hosting of Al-Qaeda and its proclaimed possession of WMDs. It also aimed at blocking Iran from acquiring nuclear weapons in addition to weakening Hezbollah and Syria. To put it differently, the states and groups, which had been perceived as threats to Israel's security and staunch supporters of Palestinians, became threats to the US as well after 9/11. Thus, AIPAC had to take these new circumstances as a golden opportunity to advance and realize their agenda through influencing US foreign policy in the MENA area. The question is: Has AIPAC succeeded in attaining this goal?

Bush and Obama Versus AIPAC: The Battle Over Shaping the Palestinian-Israeli Conflict

The Bush Administration Versus AIPAC: A Continuous Battle

The Post-9/11 Era: Bush's First Failure to Find a Compromise and AIPAC's First Victory

Being aware of the increasing anti-American feelings in the MENA region because of the US position on the Palestinian-Israeli conflict in general and its reaction to Israel's use of violence against the Palestinians during the second Intifada, the Bush Administration tried to appease these feelings through an attempt to endorse the Palestinians' right to have their own state and convince Ariel Sharon to terminate Israel's plans to build

100   F. TOUZANI

new settlements and withdraw Israeli forces from the occupied territories they broke into in October 2001.

Sharon refused Bush's request stating that Bush was attempting to appease Arabs at Israel's expense in order to garner their support on the war on terror.[59] The tension between Bush and Sharon intensified in late October 2001, which generated an unprecedented confrontation between Israel and the US.[60] Meanwhile, AIPAC drafted a statement to prompt Bush to refrain from his request and denounce his proposal of a Palestinian state because it would "reward rather than punish those who harbor and support terrorists".[61]

At the same time, AIPAC was inciting members of Congress to exert a similar pressure on Bush through meeting them and playing a leading role in helping 89 senators to draft and send a letter to Bush on November 16, 2001.[62] The letter commanded the President's refusal to meet with Arafat until the Palestinians stop attacking Israel. Additionally, the letter's signatories asked Bush to openly declare that the US was staunchly supporting Israel's right to avenge the Palestinian violence.[63]

By the end of November, the tension between the US and Israel was mollified and the bilateral relations ameliorated noticeably. Indeed, this was partly because of AIPAC's endeavors. However, it was also because of the US incipient triumph in Afghanistan, which minimized the need for Arabs to cope with Al-Qaeda. In early December, Sharon met Bush in the White House few days after the violent Israeli attacks on Gaza. The attacks were neither condemned by Bush nor did he ask Sharon to stop further attacks. In contrast, Bush asked Arafat to stop the Palestinian

---

[59] Alan Sipress and Lee Hockstader, "Sharon's Speech Riles US," *The Washington Post*, October 6, 2001. https://www.washingtonpost.com/archive/politics/2001/10/06/sha ron-speech-riles-us/97933281-c83f-4447-8d5b-540635004cae/. Accessed April 9, 2020.

[60] Suzanne Goldenberg, "Sharon Defies US Demand to Retreat," *The Guardian*, October 24, 2001.

[61] Quoted in Barbara Ferguson, "Jewish Groups Assail Bush for Endorsing Palestinian State," *Arab News*, October 13, 2001, https://www.arabnews.com/node/215457. Accessed April 10, 2020.

[62] Elaine Sciolino, "Senators Urge Bush Not to Hamper Israel," *New York Times*, November 17, 2001, https://www.nytimes.com/2001/11/17/world/senators-urge-bush-not-to-hamper-israel.html. Accessed April 10, 2020.

[63] David Singer and Lawrence Grossman, *American Jewish Year Book 2002* (American Jewish Committee: Springer, 2003), Vol. 102, p. 169.

4 INTEREST GROUPS: AN IMPERFECT IMPACT   101

use of violence against Israel.[64] In a short statement before the meeting, Bush ended the statement with "May God bless the Israeli citizens who lost their lives, and their families", with no mention of the Palestinians who lost their lives in the same struggle.[65]

The Pre-Iraq War Era: Bush's Second Failure to Find a Compromise and AIPAC's Second Triumph
Almost the same scenario was repeated by the end of March 2002 when Ariel Sharon, as a response to Hamas attacks on Israel, reoccupied almost all Palestinian-controlled territories in the West Bank and refused to withdraw upon Bush's urgent request.[66] Bush was worried about the negative impact of the Israeli actions on his image in the Middle East, especially pertaining to his plans to garner support on the war against Iraq.

AIPAC swiftly started to mobilize pro-Israel Congressional leaders from the Republican party to take action. On April 10, Tom DeLay, the House Republican Majority Leader, and Trent Lott, the Senate Republican Majority Leader, met Bush in the White House to explain the pressure put on Republicans and ask him to refrain from asking Israel to pull out.[67] One week later, Bush issued a statement in which he described Sharon as "a man of peace" and stated that Sharon responded to his request by fully and immediately withdrawing.[68] This was not the case as the Israeli forces did not fully withdraw from the West Bank and they started their partial withdrawal few days after Bush's statement.

[64] George W. Bush, "President Condemns Jerusalem Bombings," The White House, December 1, 2001, https://georgewbush-whitehouse.archives.gov/news/releases/2001/12/20011202-1.html. Accessed April 10, 2020.

[65] "George Bush Statement Before Meeting Ariel, Sharon," The White House, December 2, 2001, https://georgewbush-whitehouse.archives.gov/news/releases/2001/12/20011202-2.html. Accessed April 10, 2020.

[66] Keith B. Richburg and Molly Moore, "Israel Rejects Demands to Withdraw Troops," The Washington Post, April 11, 2002, https://www.washingtonpost.com/archive/politics/2002/04/11/israel-rejects-demands-to-withdraw-troops/7c57b427-4ac3-4f43-a88b-b22a336e30cf/. Accessed April 10, 2020.

[67] Romesh Ratnesar, "The Right's New Crusade: Lobbying for Israel," CNN, April 29, 2002, http://edition.cnn.com/ALLPOLITICS/time/2002/05/06/crusade.html. Accessed April 10, 2020.

[68] George Bush and Collin Powell, "President Bush, Secretary Powell Discuss Middle East," White House, Office of the Press Secretary, April 18, 2002, https://georgewbush-whitehouse.archives.gov/news/releases/2002/04/20020418-3.html. Accessed April 10, 2020.

102   F. TOUZANI

In the meantime, AIPAC facilitated Netanyahu's visit to Congress during which he addressed and met 40 of its senators in April to justify Israel's occupation of the West Bank and advocate for Arafat's involvement in terrorism.[69] Two weeks later, Congress passed two resolutions by an overwhelming majority to set Bush's objections aside, reassure Israel of Congress support in a common struggle against terrorism, describe Arafat as a key element of Palestinian terrorism, and provide additional appropriations for Israel to combat terrorism.[70]

The House resolution (H.Res.392) was sponsored by the Christian Zionist Republican Rep. Tom DeLay. As for the senate resolution (S.Res.247), it was sponsored by the Jewish Democrat, Sen. Joseph Lieberman. This shows an overwhelming bipartisan consensus and triumph over Bush and his administration. Rep. Tom Delay was ranked among the top ten recipients of pro-Israel PAC money in the 2004 congressional elections.[71] As for Sen. Joseph Lieberman, he received $2,001,324 between 1989 and 2014 from pro-Israel PACs and individuals.[72]

Bush and the Road Map: Sharon's Reluctance and the President's Insignificant Victories

Despite his failure in the previous two cases, Bush insisted on continuing to advocate for the establishment of a Palestinian State as he believed that it served US national interests. He pushed for the Road Map proposal

[69] CNN Transcripts, "Former Prime Minister Benjamin Netanyahu Addresses Congress," *CNN*, April 10, 2002, http://edition.cnn.com/TRANSCRIPTS/0204/10/se.02.html. Accessed April 10, 2020.

[70] H.Res.392, "Expressing Solidarity with Israel in Its Fight Against Terrorism," May 2, 2002 https://www.congress.gov/bill/107th-congress/house-resolution/392. This resolution was passed by 352–21.

S.Res.247, "A Resolution Expressing Solidarity with Israel in Its Fight Against Terrorism," April 22, 2002.

https://www.congress.gov/bill/107th-congress/senate-resolution/247. This resolution was passed by 94–2.

[71] Hugh Galford, "Pro-Israel PAC Contributions to 2004 Congressional Candidates," *Washington Report on Middle East Affairs*, July–August 2004, https://www.wrmea.org/004-july-august/004-top-ten-career-recipients-of-pro-israel-pac-funds.html. Accessed April 27, 2020.

[72] Center for Responsive Politics, Sen. Joe Lieberman (1989–2014), https://www.opensecrets.org/members-of-congress/summary?cid=N00000616&cycle=CAREER&type=I. Accessed April 27, 2020.

4 INTEREST GROUPS: AN IMPERFECT IMPACT   103

which was refused by Sharon and the Israel lobby in the US. AIPAC helped draft a letter for Congress asking the President not to pressure Israel about the Road Map. Instead, AIPAC urged Bush to put pressure on the Palestinians to abide by the security measures dictated on them.[73]

Israel seemed unmotivated about Bush's Road Map. This lack of motivation. was justified by its plan to build a "security fence", or what others called "separation barrier". This wall aimed at seizing more land from the already occupied territories in the West Bank and exposing thousands of Palestinians to more daily sufferings.[74] On July 25, 2003, Bush began to voice out his disagreement with Sharon's plan at a joint press conference in the White House with the Palestinian leader, Mahmoud Abbas. Bush considered the wall a "problem" and an impediment to developing trust between the two countries.[75]

Less than a week later, Bush welcomed Sharon to the White House. Sharon was firm on his plan to build the wall, which was not criticized by Bush, He seconded Sharon's claim that Palestinian terrorism remained the major stumbling block to peace.[76] By the end of November, Bush decided to punish Israel on its wall plan through rescinding about 10% of the $3 billion loan guarantees offered to Israel in early 2003.[77] AIPAC did not bother lobbying strongly against this decision because this meant cutting no penny from the regular US foreign aid to Israel. Rather, it

---

[73] This letter was signed by 283 representatives and 85 senators. See Nathan Guttman, "Senators, Congressmen Put Pro-Israel Stance in Writing," *Haaretz*, April 18, 2003, https://www.haaretz.com/1.4682655. Accessed April 11, 2020.

[74] This is a map of the fence, which was provided by an Israeli human rights organization called B'TSELEM.
https://www.btselem.org/download/separation_barrier_map_eng.pdf. Accessed April 11, 2020.

[75] "Remarks by George W. Bush and Mahmoud Abbas", The White House: Office of the Secretary, July 25, 2003.
https://georgewbush-whitehouse.archives.gov/news/releases/2003/07/20030725-6.html Accessed April 11, 2020.

[76] "President Discusses Middle East Peace with Prime Minister Sharon," The White House: Office of the Secretary, July 29, 2003, https://georgewbush-whitehouse.archives.gov/news/releases/2003/07/20030729-2.html. Accessed April 11, 2020.

[77] U Stephen, "US Rescinds Part of Loan Guarantees to Israel," *New York Times*, November 26, 2003, https://www.nytimes.com/2003/11/26/world/us-rescinds-part-of-loan-guarantees-to-israel.html. Accessed April 11, 2020.

104 F. TOUZANI

meant that Israel had to pay an extra $4 million each year for interest rates.[78]

The Bush administration was able to win a second minor victory over the Israel Lobby when Bush did not accept Sharon's menace to banish and force Arafat out of the West Bank in September 2003.[79] Sharon reneged and AIPAC did not do much about this issue.

The Bush Administration's Renewed Attempt to Play the Mediator: Another Failure

The re-election of Bush in November 2004 coincided with the death of Arafat in the same month. This was followed by the election of Mahmoud Abbas in January 2005 and Ehud Olmert in January 2006. Many changes in leadership, but no progress in the peace process.

Despite Abbas' recognition of Israel and his denouncement of violence from the Palestinian side as well as his passion to revitalize the peace process, Bush chose to disengage from reviving the Road Map from his re-election until late 2006. This has weakened Abbas and resulted in an unprecedented political triumph of Hamas in the 2006 elections. The Israel lobby supported this change in Bush's policy because this meant that Israel would continue to control large territories in the West Bank.[80]

The deteriorating living conditions of the Palestinians, caused by Israel's isolation of Gaza, prompted Hamas to attack Israel. The attack resulted in holding an Israeli soldier hostage in the summer of 2006. As a response, Israel reinvades Gaza. In the same summer, the situation worsened with holding two other Israeli soldiers hostage by Hezbollah. In the midst of these circumstances, the Bush administration felt obliged to advocate for resuming peace negotiations in order to guarantee a continuous Arab support on the War in Iraq as well as in Iran's attempts to acquire a nuclear arm.

The Bush administration's decision to play the intermediary coincided with a Saudi peace initiative which was adopted by the Arab League and

[78] Ibid.

[79] James Bennet, "Israel Announces Official Decision to Remove Arafat", *New York Times*, September 12, 2003, https://www.nytimes.com/2003/09/12/world/israel-announces-official-decision-to-remove-arafat.html. Accessed April 12, 2020.

[80] Ori Nir, "Influential American Jewish Coalition Balks at Endorsing Sharon's Gaza Plan," *Forward*, October 22, 2004, http://old.forward.com/articles/4361/influential-american-jewish-coalition-balks-at-end/default.htm. Accessed April 13, 2020.

4 INTEREST GROUPS: AN IMPERFECT IMPACT   105

was endorsed by the US. However, Ehud Olmert rejected most of the initiative's clauses.[81] Condoleezza Rice, US Secretary of State, met with 15 heads of US Jewish organizations, including AIPAC, to assure them that the US will exert no pressure on Israel to accept the Arab League Peace Initiative.[82]

The last decision taken by Bush before leaving office was his full support to Israel's war against Hamas in late 2008. This was a foregone conclusion because Hamas was already on the US list of terrorist groups.

The Obama Administration Versus AIPAC: A Barely Balanced Battle

In a speech at Cairo University in June 2009, Obama stated: "For more than sixty years they've endured the pain of dislocation. Many wait in refugee camps in the West Bank, Gaza, and neighboring lands for a life of peace and security that they have never been able to lead. ... America will not turn our backs on the legitimate Palestinian aspiration for dignity, opportunity, and a state of their own".[83] As a matter of fact, there has never been an American President who voiced out the rights of Palestinians to have their own state and live a decent life in many occasions and in an emphatic manner like Obama.

Mitchell's Settlement Legacy and Obama: An Early First Confrontation with the Israel Lobby

On his second day in office, Obama appointed George Mitchell as his special envoy for Middle East peace. This appointment was received with hope by most Palestinians because of Mitchell's record in calling for the freeze of Israel's illegal settlements during Bush's first term.[84] Indeed,

---

[81] Steven Erlanger, "Olmert Rejects Right of Return for Palestinians," *New York Times*, March 31, 2007, https://www.nytimes.com/2007/03/31/world/middleeast/31mideast. html. Accessed April 13, 2020.

[82] Ron Kampeas, "Rice Focuses on Endgame," The Jewish Telegraphic Agency, February 11, 2007, https://www.jta.org/2007/02/11/united-states/rice-focuses-on-end game. Accessed April 13, 2020.

[83] Barack Obama, "Remarks by the President on a New Beginning," Cairo University(Egypt), June 4, 2009, https://obamawhitehouse.archives.gov/the-press-office/rem arks-president-cairo-university-6-04-09. Accessed April 14, 2020.

[84] Sharm El-Sheikh Fact-Finding Committee Report "Mitchell Report," April 30, 2001, http://eeas.europa.eu/archives/docs/mepp/docs/mitchell_report_2001_en. pdf. Accessed April 14, 2020.

106   F. TOUZANI

Mitchell's recommendation was adopted by the Obama Administration and was translated into an energetic and a clear statement in May 2009 by Secretary of State, Hillary Clinton. Clinton stated that the President "wants to see a stop to settlements—not some settlements, not outposts, not natural growth exceptions".[85] Obama started with the problem of settlement because he believed that it would hinder a potential progress in achieving peace.

This statement sparked AIPAC's worries and swiftly responded by mobilizing Congress to send a letter to Obama to urge him to work "closely and privately" with Israel and not exert public pressure on it on the issue of settlement.[86] The letter was signed by 329 representatives and 76 senators. They all called for maintaining the status quo and stated that the US "must be both a trusted mediator and devoted friend of Israel".[87]

Obama seemed to get the message from Congress that the Israeli lobby is dissatisfied with his pressure on Israel and the perceived shift in US foreign policy toward this country. Consequently, he met with representatives of 14 US Jewish organizations, including AIPAC, to appease them and explain the perceived "evenhandedness" among Jewish leaders vis-a-vis Israel. Obama confirmed this perception and responded saying: "you are absolutely right and we are going to fix that… the sense of evenhandedness has to be restored".[88] In fact, this statement sounds like an implicit apology to the Israel Lobby.

Furthermore, Obama appointed Dennis Ross as the Special Assistant to the President and Senior Director for the Central Region, which includes the Middle East and the Gulf in addition to Pakistan, Afghanistan, and

---

[85] Martin S. Indyk, Kenneth G. Lieberthal and Michael E. O'Hanlon, *Bending History: Barack Obama's Foreign Policy* (Brookings Institution Press, 2012), p. 119.

[86] Ben Smith, "Dems pressure Obama on Israel," *Politico*, June 1, 2009, https://www.politico.com/story/2009/06/dems-pressure-obama-on-israel-023207. Accessed April 14, 2002.

[87] Chris McGreal, "US pro-Israeli Group Attempts to Stop Shift in White House Middle East Policy: AIPAC Urges Congress Members to Sign Letter to Barack Obama Calling for Israel to Set Pace of Negotiations with Palestinian," *The Guardian*, May 6, 2009, https://www.theguardian.com/world/2009/may/06/us-israel-palestinians-middle-east. Accessed April 14, 2020.

[88] Josh Ruebner, *Shattered Hopes: Obama's Failure to Broker Israeli-Palestinian Peace* (New York: Verso, 2014), p. 281.

South Asia.[89] As a Jew and a staunch pro-Israel politician, Ross had no affinity to Mitchell. In fact, Ross ignored Mitchell when this latter was conducting negotiations with Israeli officials.[90]

To counterbalance the appointment of Dennis Ross, Obama appointed Chuck Hagel as the US Secretary of Defense in 2013. This appointment showed a limitation to AIPAC's influence on executive appointments taking into consideration that Hagel was very critical of Israel and AIPAC in particular.[91]

Despite the fact that Obama was able to wheedle Israel to partially freeze its settlements in 2009 and 2010, the total number of settlements during his presidency exceeded that of his predecessor's according to data presented by Israel's Central Bureau of Statistics and Peace Now, an anti-settlement watchdog organization.[92]

The Israeli Settlements and Obama's Stance in the United Nations: When a Tie Has a Taste of Defeat

Surprisingly enough and unlike Obama's initial emphatic call for Israel to stop all kinds of settlements in the West Bank, the US, under his direction, vetoed an anti-settlement UN Security Council resolution in February 2011. The resolution was backed by all members including the UK and

---

[89] Glenn Kessler, "Dennis Ross Is Moved from State Department Post to White House," *The Washington Post*, June 15, 2009, http://voices.washingtonpost.com/44/2009/06/15/dennis_ross_is_moved_from_stat.html. Accessed April 14, 2020.

[90] Barak Ravid and Natasha Mozgovaya, "Obama's Mideast Adviser Steps Down Amid Stalled Peace Talks," *Haaretz*, November 10, 2011, https://www.haaretz.com/1.520 8428. Accessed April 14, 2020.

[91] Chris McGreal, "Chuck Hagel Not Antisemitic for Saying Pro-Israel Lobby Has a Powerful Voice," *The Guardian*, January 7, 2013, https://www.theguardian.com/world/2013/jan/07/chuck-hagel-not-antisemitic-israel. Accessed April 16, 2020.

[92] Josef Federman, "Israeli Settlements Have Grown During the Obama Years," *APNews*, September 16, 2016, https://apnews.com/93e1597c5da7493ea49c29260f7f8004/israeli-settlements-have-grown-during-obama-years. Accessed April 14, 2020.

108   F. TOUZANI

France.[93] AIPAC praised Obama's use of veto to block an attempt to condemn and delegitimize Israel's settlement.[94]

Unlike the 2011 UN resolution, Obama decided to take a different stance on a similar UN Security Council resolution 2334 in 2016. The US abstained from voting unlike the 14 other members which voted in favor of the resolution.[95] The US abstention allowed the resolution to pass, which made the Israeli settlements illegal according to the international law.[96]

AIPAC reacted to the US abstention stating that it was "deeply disturbed by the failure of the Obama administration to exercise its veto to prevent a destructive, one-sided, anti-Israel resolution from being enacted by the United Nations Security Council".[97] Before the adoption of the resolution, AIPAC created a platform in their website in order to mobilize Americans to urge their federal representatives in Congress to thank those who spoke against it and urge those who did not in an attempt to put pressure on Obama to veto it in the UN.[98] Indeed, a large and a very significant group of 387 members of Congress sent a letter to Obama to urge him to veto UNSC resolution 2334.[99] Despite this pressure, Obama was determined to win this battle over AIPAC less than a month before the end of his second term.

[93] "United States Vetoes Security Council Resolution on Israeli Settlements," *United Nations News*, February 19, 2011, https://news.un.org/en/story/2011/02/367082-uni ted-states-vetoes-security-council-resolution-israeli-settlements. Accessed April 14, 2020.

[94] Hilary Leila Krieger, "US Vetoes UN Resolution Condemning Settlements as Illegal," *The Jerusalem Post*, February 19, 2011, https://m.jpost.com/International/US-vetoes-UN-resolution-condemning-settlements-as-illegal Accessed April 15, 2020.

[95] "UN Security Council Resolution 2334," The United Nations, December 23, 2016, https://www.un.org/webcast/pdfs/SRES2334-2016.pdf. Accessed April 15, 2020.

[96] Ibid.

[97] "AIPAC Statement on U.S. Abstention from UNSC Resolution Vote," December 23, 2016, https://www.aipac.org/resources/aipac-publications/publication?pubpath=Pol icyPolitics/Press/AIPAC%20Statements/2016/12/AIPAC%20Statement%20on%20US% 20Abstention%20from%20UNSC%20Resolution%20Vote. Accessed April 15, 2020.

[98] Eric Cortellessa, "AIPAC Looks to Push Congress on Opposition to UN Resolution," *The Times of Israel*, December 30, 2016, https://www.timesofisrael.com/aipac-looks-to-push-congress-on-opposition-to-un-resolution/. Accessed April 1, 2020.

[99] Letter to President Obama from Members of Congress about UNSC Resolution 2334, April 13, 2016, https://lieu.house.gov/sites/lieu.house.gov/files/documents/ Lowey%20Granger%20Final%20Letter%20%283%29.pdf. Accessed April 15, 2020.

4 INTEREST GROUPS: AN IMPERFECT IMPACT 109

The Statehood of Palestine and Obama's Stance in the UN:
A Last-Minute Shift Again
In September 2011 and after a two-year stalemate in peace negotiations
with Israel, Mahmoud Abbas decided to apply for state membership to
the United Nations. In case of admission, it would allow Palestine to take
legal proceedings against Israel and other countries in the International
Criminal Court (ICC). To be a full member of the UN, Palestine had
to be recommended by the Security Council. Then, it has to gain the
support of two thirds of the General Assembly. While gaining the two-
third majority in the General Assembly was not a big challenge, it was
almost impossible to get the Security Council's recommendation because
the US would more likely block it through the use of the veto.[100]

Therefore, the Palestinians chose an easier option. That is, to become
a "non-member state", which necessitates a simple majority in the
General Assembly. Indeed, this option would still recognize the statehood of Palestine. On November 29, 2012, Palestine was recognized as
a "non-member observer state" by the GA resolution 67/19. This resolution required using the appellation of "State of Palestine" in all UN
documents.[101]

Before the adoption of the GA resolution, AIPAC played a key role
in mobilizing its friends in Congress to pass a series of bills to reject and
block the initiative. threaten to suspend aid to Palestinians and put pressure on Obama to veto it, which he did.[102] This included a House bill
H.Res.1765 which was sponsored by Rep. Howard Berman.[103] Berman
was a Jewish Zionist who once stated "even before I was a Democrat,

---

[100] As of July 2019, the State of Palestine was recognized by 138 member states of
the UN, which is more than two thirds of the total number (193 member states). See
Permanent à observer Mission of the State Of Palestine to the United Nations (New York)
https://palestineun.org/about-palestine/diplomatic-relations/. Accessed April 16, 2020.

[101] United Nations General Assembly Resolution 67/19, Status of Palestine Status in
the United à Nations, December 4, 2012, https://unispal.un.org/UNISPAL.NSF/0/198
62D03C564FA2C85257ACB004EE69B. Accessed April 16, 2020.

[102] AIPAC, "Condemn Palestinian Recognition at UN". Accessed April 16, 2020.
https://www.aipac.org/learn/legislative-agenda/agenda-display?agendaid=%7BD287
37B1-8EEC-4339-BF9B-B357733A48C8%7D.

[103] H.Res.1765 (111th Congress), "Supporting a negotiated solution to the Israeli-
Palestinian conflict and condemning unilateral measures to declare or recognize a
Palestinian state, and for other purposes", December 15, 2010, https://www.congress.
gov/bill/111th-congress/house-resolution/1765/text. Accessed April 16, 2020.

110   F. TOUZANI

I was a Zionist".[104] Ari Goldberg, who was working as a staffer for Howard Berman, was later appointed as AIPAC's spokesman.[105] The Senate passed a bill, S.Res.185 which was introduced by Sen. Benjamin Cardin, a Jew and one of the closest Democrats to AIPAC according to the Times of Israel.[106]

Just like he did with the anti-settlements UN resolution, Obama seemed to reconsider his position again about the statehood of Palestine toward the end of his eight-year tenure. Obama refused to make a public statement to oppose the "Palestinian Statehood Bid" upon requests from Senator Minority Leader Harry Reid who was told twice that the White House is reassessing its position about this issue.[107] This shift in Obama's opinion was mainly attributed to a statement by Benjamin Netanyahu in which he emphatically stated that he would block any attempt to make the statehood of Palestine a reality.[108]

Bush, and Obama Versus AIPAC: The Ultimate Triumph of Diplomacy on the Iran Nuclear Program

After defeating Saddam Hussein's regime in Iraq, Iran emerged as the strongest challenge to the US and Israel in the region owing to two major factors. First, Iran's potential development of nuclear weapons may threaten Israel's security as well as the US forces based in the region. Second, Iran has a great prospect of controlling the oil-rich region due to its strong bonds with the Shia in Iraq, Hezbollah in Lebanon, and the Houthis in Yemen. Therefore, it is very important for the US and Israel to prevent Iran from going nuclear and dominating the Middle East.

---

[104] Nathan Guttman, "New Foreign Affairs Committee Chairman Draws Praise From Sides," *Forward*, April 24, 2008, https://forward.com/news/13244/new-foreign-affairs-committee-chairman-draws-prais-01741/. Accessed April 16, 2020.

[105] Ron Kampeas, "AIPAC Bringing in a New Spokesman," Jewish Telegraph Agency, February 7, 2011, https://www.jta.org/2011/02/07/united-states/aipac-bringing-in-a-new-spokesman. Accessed April 16, 2020.

[106] JTA, "AIPAC-aligned Senator Cardin to address J Street Confab," *The Times of Israel*, March 22, 2018, https://www.timesofisrael.com/aipac-aligned-senator-cardin-to-address-j-street-confab/. Accessed April 16, 2020.

[107] John Bresnahan and Edward-Isaac Dovere, "Exclusive: Obama brushed off Reid's Plea on Palestinian State," *Politico*, October 1, 2015, https://www.politico.com/story/2015/10/reid-obama-israel-palestinians-netanyahu-united-nations-214011. Accessed April 16, 2020.

[108] Ibid.

There are two different approaches to achieving this goal. The first one is publicly advocated for by Israel and equivocally supported by the Israel lobby in the US. This approach favors the use of forceful means such as economic sanctions or a military intervention. Proponents of this approach minimize the effectiveness of diplomatic measures and economic incentives to prevent Iran from acquiring a nuclear arm. This strategy necessitates maintaining a permanent and a strong US military presence in the region. The second approach to dealing with Iran's nuclear program is to engage in diplomatic negotiations with this country. This approach necessitates eliminating the option of using force because it would make the Iranian leaders more zealous about seeking a deterrent arm.

The Bush Administration and AIPAC on Iran's Nuclear Program: When National and International Factors Restrict the Lobby's Influence

The Use of Force Against Iran: When the Public Opinion Restrains the Lobby's Public Rhetoric

Iran was part of Bush's "axis of evil". The axis was identified after September 11 and included Iraq and North Korea because of these countries' alleged sponsorship of terrorism or their development of weapons of mass destruction. After the collapse of Saddam's regime, Israel began its advocacy for a regime change in Iran because of this country's potential intention to develop a nuclear weapon.[109]

Bush's rhetoric mirrored that of Israel's in many speeches including the one he delivered in March 2006:

> The threat is, of course, their stated objective to destroy our strong ally Israel. That's a threat, a serious threat ... I made it clear, I'll make it clear again, that we will use military might to protect our ally, Israel.[110]

Some members of the Israeli lobby requested the White House to abstain from making public statements about the US determination to

---

[109] Stephen Farrell, Robert Thomson, and Danielle Haas, "Attack Iran the Day Iraq War Ends, Demands Israel," *Times* (London), November 5, 2002, https://www.thetimes.co.uk/article/attack-iran-the-day-iraq-war-ends-demands-israel-j0kqj6tpczz. Accessed April 17, 2020.

[110] Quoted in John P. McTernan, *As America Has Done To Israel* (Whitaker House, 2008), p. 242.

112 F. TOUZANI

use force against Iran to defend Israel. The Jewish community in the US believed that such public statements might be blamed for the negative repercussions of a possible military attack against Iran, especially in a moment when Bush was encountering an increasing criticism about the war on Iraq.[111]

The Israeli lobby's request can be explained by the fact that the US public opinion was strongly opposing the military option. According to a 2007 opinion poll conducted by US Today/Gallup Poll, 73% of Americans favored diplomatic and economic means to force Iran to stop its nuclear plan while 18% only preferred the military option.[112]

Unlike AIPAC's rank-and-file members, the option of waging war on Iran was not advocated for by AIPAC's leadership in its 2007 policy conference during which AIPAC's policy convictions are usually voiced out. None of AIPAC's leaders openly talked about war with Iran in their speeches or during panel discussions. On the other hand, very few well-known external speakers did.[113] One of the few prominent external leaders who called for a forceful approach to dealing with Iran's nuclear ambitions was Pastor John Hagee, the well-known Christian Zionist and the founder of one of the staunchest pro-Israel US organizations. Namely, Christians United For Israel (CUFI). John Hagee stated:

> it is 1938; Iran is Germany and Ahmadinejad is the new Hitler. Ladies and gentlemen we must stop Iran's nuclear threat and stop it now and stand boldly with Israel, the only democracy in the Middle East. The only way to win a nuclear war is to make certain it never starts.[114]

---

[111] Ori Nir, "Groups to Bush: Drop Iran-Israel Linkage," *Forward*, May 12, 2006, https://forward.com/news/1386/groups-to-bush-drop-iran-israel-linkage/. Accessed April 17, 2020.

[112] Lydia Saad, "Americans Want a Restrained Iran Strategy," *Gallup Poll*, November 6, 2007, https://news.gallup.com/poll/102592/americans-want-restrained-iran-strategy.aspx. Accessed April 19, 2020.

[113] Gregory Levey, "Inside America's Powerful Israel Lobby," *Salon*, March 16, 2007, https://www.salon.com/2007/03/16/aipac/. Accessed April 18, 2020.

[114] John Hagee, "Speech at AIPAC Policy Conference 2007," March 11, 2007, https://www.aipac.org/-/media/publications/policy-and-politics/speeches-and-int erviews/speeches-by-policymakers/2007/03/hagee_pc_2007.pdf. Accessed April 18, 2007.

4 INTEREST GROUPS: AN IMPERFECT IMPACT   113

John Hagee was given the privilege to speak at the opening plenary dinner of the 2007 AIPAC's policy conference. Hagee was very warmly welcomed and his speech was strongly and frequently applauded by a crowd of about 6000 AIPAC delegates. In brief, it is difficult to assess the influence of AIPAC on Bush's discourse to use force against Iran because of its leaders' ambiguous position on this issue and the role of public opinion in this regard.

The Imposition of Sanctions on Iran: When an International Factor Facilitates the Lobby's Influence
With a very minimal reference to Israel, Bush's frequent threats of using force seemed useless in deterring Iran from pursuing its nuclear plan. As a result, Bush thought about an alternative means. That is to say, the imposition of economic sanctions.

In June 2005, Bush issued an executive order 13,382 to freeze the properties of individuals involved in Iran's nuclear program.[115] Furthermore, he took advantage of the International Atomic Energy Agency's (IAEA) report of Iran's non-compliance with its restrictions on uranium enrichment to start advocating for international sanctions. In December 2006, March 2007, and March 2008, Bush was able to persuade all members of the Security Council to impose sanctions on Iran and toughen them after refusing to close its nuclear installations.[116]

Meanwhile, AIPAC was advocating for similar sanctions in Congress through their pro-Israel members. To illustrate, the House passed a bill (H.R.1400) titled "Iran Counter Proliferation Act of 2007". 397

---

[115] George W. Bush Executive Order 13,382, the US Department of Treasury, June 28, 2005, https://www.treasury.gov/resource-center/sanctions/Programs/Documents/wmd. pdf. Accessed April 20, 2020.

[116] "Security Council Imposes Sanctions on Iran for Failure to Half Uranium Enrichment, Unanimously Adopting Resolution 1737", Press Release: The United Nations Security Council, December 23, 2006, https://www.un.org/press/en/2006/sc8928.doc. htm; "Security Council Tightens Sanctions Against Iran Over Uranium Enrichment," *The United Nations News*, March 24, 2007, https://news.un.org/en/story/2007/03/213372-security-council-tightens-sanctions-against-iran-over-uranium-enrichment; "Security Council Restrictions on Iran's Proliferation-Sensitive Nuclear Activities, Increases Vigilance over Iranian Banks, Inspect Cargo," The United Nations News, March 3, 2008, https://www.un.org/press/en/2008/sc9268.doc.htm. Accessed April 17, 2020.

114   F. TOUZANI

members voted in favor of the bill and only 16 voted against it.[117] This bill was sponsored by the late Rep. Tom Lantos, a Holocaust survivor and AIPAC's strong ally. The bill aimed at supporting Security Council sanctions on Iran and called for toughening them. In addition, the bill called for the imposition of tough US sanctions on the same country. Lantos was of one of the top receivers of financial contributions from pro-Israel PACs most of which are affiliated with AIPAC. To illustrate, the largest amount he received from various PACs in 2000 came from pro-Israel PACs.[118]

In sum, while AIPAC exerted a strong influence on Congress to pass legislations that impose sanctions on Iran, it is difficult to talk about a similar influence on the President's decision to support international sanctions on Iran. This is because the international community, including the permanent members of the Security Council, was predisposed to accept the sanctions, especially after the IAEA's report of Iran's non-compliance with its regulations.

Clearly, neither the threats to use force nor the imposition of tough sanctions could deter Iran from its nuclear plan. The only approach which was not exhausted was the diplomatic one. This was sought by President Obama who faced a strong opposition from AIPAC.

The Obama Administration Versus AIPAC on Iran's Nuclear Program: The Triumph of Diplomacy
From a Confrontational Discourse to an Amiable Rhetoric: Obama's First Diplomatic Attempt with Iran and AIPAC's First Attempt to Influence the Negotiations
Unlike Bush's confrontational "axis-of-evil" language toward Iran, Obama started his term with conveying positive messages. Messages that display a determination to resolve the conflict with Iran through diplomatic means. In his inaugural address, Obama stated:

[117] H.R.1400 (110th Congress)- Iran Counter-Proliferation Act of 2007, September 26, 2007, https://www.congress.gov/bill/110th-congress/house-bill/1400/all-info. Accessed April 19, 2020.

[118] Center for Responsive Politics, Top contributions to Rep. Tom Lantos (1999–2000), https://www.opensecrets.org/members-of-congress/summary?cid=N00007382&cycle=2000&type=I. Accessed April 20, 2020.

4 INTEREST GROUPS: AN IMPERFECT IMPACT   115

> To the Muslim World, we seek a new way forward, based on mutual interest and mutual respect … we will extend a hand if you are willing to unclench your fist.[119]

Although the message was sent to the Muslim world, it was clear that Obama was addressing Iran in particular because it was the country with which the US had the most tensional relationship. In a more direct message two months after the inaugural speech, Obama sent a short recording to the Iranian people and leaders to congratulate them on the Persian New Year, *Nowruz*, praise Iran's rich cultural heritage, and wish Iran a bright future.[120]

After Iran's first positive response to US-Russia "fuel swap" proposal in April 2009, Obama's first diplomatic attempt to strike a deal with Iran, along with the IAEA and the other permanent members of the Security Council plus Germany (P5+1), was first delayed because of the re-election of Mahmoud Ahmadinejad in June 2009. Ahmadinejad's re-election resulted in weeks of demonstrations claiming that the elections were rigged.

In these circumstances and feeling obliged to accept Obama's diplomatic attempt, AIPAC asked Obama to grant Iran limited time to respond to the proposal. At the same time, AIPAC was lobbying members of Congress to adopt resolutions imposing the toughest sanctions possible on Iran during their 2009 policy conference. The main purpose was to deter Iran's further development of its nuclear program.[121] The 2009 policy conference strongly focused on highlighting the Iranian threats not only on Israel but also on the US and other countries.[122]

While Iran's response was largely influenced by the internal aforementioned protests, AIPAC succeeded in lobbying its supporters in Congress to introduce a bill (H.R.2194) on April 30, 2009. The bill, titled

---

[119] Barack Obama, "President Barack Obama Inaugural Address," The White House, January 21, 2009, https://obamawhitehouse.archives.gov/blog/2009/01/21/president-barack-obamas-inaugural-address. Accessed April 20, 2020.

[120] Barack Obama, "A New Year, a New Beginning," The White House, March 19, 2009, https://obamawhitehouse.archives.gov/blog/2009/03/19/a-new-year-a-new-beginning. Accessed April 20, 2020.

[121] Richard Silverstein, "AIPAC Hidden Persuaders," *The Guardian*, May 15, 2009, https://www.theguardian.com/commentisfree/cifamerica/2009/may/13/aipac-iran-us-obama. Accessed April 21, 2020.

[122] Ibid.

116   F. TOUZANI

"Comprehensive Iran Sanctions, Accountability, and Divestment Act", recommended imposing additional tougher sanctions. It stated that these sanctions are more likely to help the international diplomatic endeavors with Iran have effective results.[123]

The Bill (H.R.2194) was sponsored by Rep. Howard Berman, a Jewish Democrat and a staunch Zionist whose staffer, Ari Goldberg, was later appointed as AIPAC's spokesman.[124] Berman received $612 190 from Pro-Israel PACs between 1989 and 2014.[125] However, H.R.2194 could not take any step further until after the diplomatic negotiations with Iran were resumed in October 2009 taking into consideration that it was introduced in April 2009.[126] This means that while AIPAC may succeed in lobbying members of Congress to introduce bills in favor of Israel, introducing a bill does not always lead to a success in influencing the legislative process.

When the negotiations were resumed in October 2009, Iran declined the initial "fuel swap" proposal due to internal opposition. In fact, this was an Iranian attempt to re-negotiate the clauses of the "fuel swap". The US, along with France and Russia, refused Iran's new terms and conditions. Consequently, more sanctions were imposed on Iran by Congress and the Security Council.[127]

Iran Versus Obama: The Game of Chicken
The failure of Obama's first diplomatic attempt with Iran resulted in resorting to sanctions again both on the international and national levels. In the same vein, the Security Council adopted Resolution 1929 on June

---

[123] H.R.2194 (111th Congress)—"Comprehensive Iran Sanctions, Accountability, and Divestment Act of 2010," April 30, 2009, https://www.congress.gov/bill/111th-congress/house-bill/2194. Accessed April 21, 2020.

[124] Ibid. Notes 118 and 119.

[125] Center for Responsive Politics, Rep. Howard Berman PACs contributions (1989–2014), https://www.opensecrets.org/members-of-congress/summary?cid=N00008094&cycle=CAREER. Accessed April 21, 2020.

[126] See the path that this resolution took from its introduction to its adoption as a public law https://www.congress.gov/bill/111th-congress/house-bill/2194/actions?KWICView=false. Accessed April 21, 2020.

[127] For more details on the 'fuel swap' proposal and Iran's new suggested arrangements, see Trita Parsi, *Losing an Enemy: Obama, Iran and the Triumph of Diplomacy* (Yale University Press/New Haven & London, 2017), Chapter 6: A Single Roll of the Dice, pp. 79–103.

4 INTEREST GROUPS: AN IMPERFECT IMPACT 117

9, 2010. The resolution toughened the previously imposed sanctions including further restrictions on nuclear proliferation and test-related measures as well as a total arms embargo on exports to Iran.[128]

This international development facilitated the adoption of the previously mentioned H.R.2194 which was lobbied for by AIPAC and was passed by both the House and the Senate before being signed by Obama on July 1, 2010. This is another case showing that AIPAC's influence can be influenced by an international factor.

In response to these sanctions, Iran decided to expand its nuclear activities, especially pertaining to uranium enrichment. This ran against the fundamental goals of the US and the P5+Germany.[129] The stalemate lasted for about six months due to Iran's insistence on recognizing its right to enrich uranium and lifting sanctions as conditions to resume negotiations. On the other side, the US and its allies insisted on stopping the enrichment process to go back to negotiations. After the six-month stalemate, the parties met in December 2010 in Geneva and later in Istanbul in January 2011. However, the meetings had no new outcomes.

The second stalemate lasted for about a year. During this stalemate, Iran stayed defiant and continued its nuclear activities despite the deteriorating economic conditions which resulted from the tough sanctions and the methodic plan to isolate Iran. The worsening conditions of the Iranian economy and the US worries about Iran's threatening development of its nuclear activities prompted both parties to resume negotiations in 2012 with a series of meetings involving Iran and the P5+Germany.

The meetings started in Istanbul in April followed by another one in Baghdad in May and a third one in Moscow in June.[130] These political meetings were followed by technical ones in July, which involved experts from all parties. Meanwhile, the IAEA was issuing reports about Iran's nuclear activities in 2012. The last report was in November; it reported that Iran continued its production of uranium enriched to 20%.[131] In

---

[128] Security Council Resolution 1929, June 9, 2010 https://www.iaea.org/sites/def ault/files/unsc_res1929-2010.pdf Accessed April 21, 2020.

[129] Parsi, *Losing an Enemy*, p. 104.

[130] For more details about these meetings, see Parsi, *Losing an Enemy*, pp. 108–131.

[131] Kelsey Davenport, Daryl G. Kimball and Greg Thielmann, "The November 2012 IAEA Report on Iran and Its Implications", *Arms Control Association*, November 16, 2012, https://armscontrol.org/blog/2012-11-16/november-2012-iaea-report-iran-its-implications. Accessed April 22, 2020.

118 F. TOUZANI

April 2013, Iran and the P5+1 met to announce that the parties are far apart and no more meetings are planned.

Obama Versus AIPAC on the Iran Deal: The Final Battle

Obama and Iran's New President: The Path to JCPOA

The change of leadership in Iran seemed to bring about a glimmer of hope for the negotiations with the election of the moderate Hassan. Three days after his inauguration in August 3, 2013, Rouhani called for resuming serious negotiations with the P5+1.[132] This was a clear breakup from his predecessor, Mahmoud Ahmadinejad who was known for his confrontational rhetoric with the US in particular. Another breakup from his predecessors was Obama's phone call with Rouhani in September 2013.

Following this positive exchange, a series of meetings were held between Iran and the P5+1 with the IAEA's involvement. Despite the few stumbling blocks that hindered the negotiations, a deal was finally reached and the Joint Comprehensive Plan Of Action (JCPOA) was signed in Vienna on July 14, 2015 few months before the end of Obama's second term. Under this agreement, Iran agreed to restrict its nuclear activities, including uranium enrichment, and put them under the IAEA's inspection in return for putting an end to the sanctions.[133] The Iran nuclear deal sparked a strong criticism and refusal from AIPAC during the negotiations and after it was finalized.

AIPAC's Sanctions vs Obama's Diplomacy: The Major Pre-deal Combat

AIPAC began its lobbying efforts in Congress to block the negotiations in December 2013 less than three months after they were resumed. It mobilized about 10,000 of its lobbyists to put pressure on legislators to support a new bill (S.1881) introduced by Sensor Robert

---

[132] "Iran's New Leader Rouhani Urges 'Serious' Nuclear Talks," *BBC News*, August 6, 2013, https://www.bbc.com/news/world-middle-east-23591371. Accessed April 22, 2020.

[133] Joint Comprehensive Plan of Action, July 14, 2015, https://www.europarl.europa.eu/cmsdata/122460/full-text-of-the-iran-nuclear-deal.pdf. Accessed April 22, 2020.

4 INTEREST GROUPS: AN IMPERFECT IMPACT   119

Menendez.[134] Sen. Menendez is a staunch supporter of Israel. He was awarded the Political Courage honor by the American Friends of the right-wing Israel political party, Likud (AFL) in May 2014. The award was given few months after he sponsored and introduced the bill.[135] From 2015 to 2020, Menendez received $580 272 from pro-Israel PACs and individuals.[136]

The bill, titled the "Nuclear Weapon Free Iran Act of 2013", aimed at reducing Iran's oil revenues, supporting Israel in case it is obliged to defend itself against nuclear Iran and commanded Obama to impose a zero-enrichment clause on Iran.[137] It is clear that this bill would have harmed the negotiations in their beginnings had it been passed. That is why Obama vowed to veto the bill and other potential similar bills in his State of the Union Address of 2014 and insisted on diplomacy to deal with Iran.[138] In any rate, the bill did not make it to a vote due to the support of the US National Security Council and the US intelligence. Both entities argued that new sanctions would undermine the negotiations and may leave the US with one option; that is, the use of force because the use of sanctions seemed not to work with Iran.[139]

Because of the terrible repercussions of the war on Iraq and the civil war in Syria, it was very difficult for America to wage another war in the

[134] Rebecca Shimoni Stoil, "AIPAC Offers Senate Democrats a Way Out on Iran," *The Times of Israel*, March 2, 2014, https://www.timesofisrael.com/aipac-offers-senate-democrats-a-way-out-on-iran/. Accessed April 22, 2020.

[135] Adam Fishman, "Senator Bob Menendez Outlines Positions on Israel, Iran," *The Algemeiner*, May 26, 2014, https://www.algemeiner.com/2014/05/26/senator-bob-menendez-outlines-positions-on-israel-iran/. Accessed April 23, 2020.

[136] Center for Responsive Politics, Sen. Robert Menendez PACs Contributions (2015–2020) https://www.opensecrets.org/members-of-congress/summary?cid=N00000699. Accessed April 24, 2020.

[137] S.1881 (113th Congress)—Nuclear Weapon Free Iran Act of 2013, December 20, 2013, https://www.congress.gov/bill/113th-congress/senate-bill/1881. Accessed April 22, 2020.

[138] Barack Obama, "State of the Union Address," The White House, January 28, 2014, https://obamawhitehouse.archives.gov/the-press-office/2014/01/28/president-barack-obamas-state-union-address, Accessed April 23, 2020.

[139] Paul Richter, "White House Suggests Iran Sanctions Bill Could Draw U.S. into War," *Los Angelos Times*, January 10, 2014, https://www.latimes.com/world/worldnow/la-fg-wn-white-house-iran-nuclear-deal-20140110-story.html. Accessed April 23, 2020.

region. This case resulted in a humiliating defeat of AIPAC and a very significant triumph of Obama's diplomatic approach.

In fact, the failure of S.1881 was the major card which AIPAC pushed and advocated for to hinder the negotiations. Obama reiterated his determination to veto similar bills because sanctions proved unsuccessful. Moreover, if diplomacy fails, the US would be left with one option. That is to say, waging war on Iran. Indeed, Americans were predisposed not to accept this option because of the negative experience in Iraq. This rhetoric helped Obama counter other AIPAC's initiatives aiming at impeding his diplomatic endeavors. Consequently, he was able to win the battle, strike the deal with Iran, and sign the Joint Comprehensive Plan Of Action (JCPOA) in Vienna on July 14, 2015. However, Obama had to win the final combat to pass the JCPOA in Congress.

The Final Battle: The Triumph of Diplomacy and AIPAC's Humiliating Defeat

The Iran Nuclear Agreement Act of 2015 was enacted as a public law on May 22, 2015. According to this act, any agreement with Iran must undergo a period of sixty-day review by Congress which can approve, disapprove, or not react to the agreement.[140] The law included additional time for the President to veto Congress decision and for Congress to sustain or override the President's veto.

To consider a resolution rejecting the deal for a vote, the opponents of the deal in the Senate had to secure 60 votes and an additional 7 votes to override Obama's veto. On the other hand, proponents of the Iran deal would have to secure 34 votes in order to protect Obama's veto in the senate. As for the House of Representatives, Obama's supporters had to secure 146 votes out of 435 votes to safeguard his veto.

The sixty-day review period began on July 20, 2015 and ended on September 17. AIPAC began its lobbying efforts in Congress immediately when its executive director, Howard Kohr, commanded his staff to cancel their summer vacations to get ready for the final combat.[141] On

---

[140] H.R.1191 (114th Congress) Iran Nuclear Agreement Review Act of 2015, May 22, 2015, https://www.congress.gov/bill/114th-congress/house-bill/1191/text. Accessed April 25, 2020.

[141] Adam Lerner, "AIPAC Forms New Group to Oppose Iran Deal," *Politico*, July 17, 2015, https://www.politico.com/story/2015/07/aipac-iran-deal-citizens-for-a-nuclear-free-iran-120307. Accessed April 25, 2020.

4 INTEREST GROUPS: AN IMPERFECT IMPACT   121

July 16, Kohr sent a phone script to tens of thousands of AIPAC's lobbyists and urged them to use it to call their representatives in Congress as well as meet them in their district offices over the summer break.[142] By August 5, AIPAC lobbyists conducted about 400 meetings with members of Congress.[143]

Furthermore, AIPAC created "Citizens for Nuclear Free Iran", an advocacy group whose goal was to inform Americans about "the dangers of the proposed Iran deal". The advisory board of this group constituted of five former Democratic members of Congress.[144] The new organization would spend between $20 and $40 million to advocate for its opposition of the Iran deal through media ads, paying for AIPAC's members flights to Washington and organizing protests at offices of members of Congress.[145]

Obama was ready for the combat. One day after the agreement was concluded, he urged Congress to endorse the deal: "If we don't choose wisely, I believe future generations will judge us harshly, for letting this moment slip away".[146] He also dedicated his weekly radio address on July 18 to advocate for the deal and criticized the opponents for not

---

[142] The script reads "I am calling to urge the senator/representative to oppose the Iran nuclear deal because it will not block Iran from getting a nuclear weapon". See Ron Kampeas, "AIPAC to fight White House head-to-head in battle over Iran deal", *The Times of Israel*, July 17, 2015, https://www.timesofisrael.com/aipac-to-fight-white-house-head-to-head-in-battle-over-iran-deal/. Accessed April 25, 2020.

[143] Ailsa Chang, "Lobbyists Spending Millions To Sway The Undecided On Iran Deal," *NPR*, August 6, 2015, https://www.npr.org/sections/itsallpolitics/2015/08/06/429911872/in-iran-deal-fight-lobbyists-are-spending-millions-to-sway-12-senators. Accessed April 26, 2020.

[144] Alexander Bolton, "New Group Backed by AIPAC Targets Deal," *The Hill*, July 17, 2015, https://thehill.com/homenews/senate/248349-new-group-backed-by-aipac-targets-iran-deal. Accessed April 25, 2020.

[145] M.J. Rosenberg, "AIPAC Spent Millions of Dollars to Defeat the Iran Deal. Instead, It May Have Destroyed Itself", *The Nation*, September 11, 2015, https://www.thenation.com/article/archive/aipac-spent-millions-of-dollars-to-defeat-the-iran-deal-instead-it-may-have-destroyed-itself/. Accessed April 25, 2020.

[146] Jordan Fabian, "Obama's Five Big Arguments on Iran Deal," *The Hill*, July 18, 2015, https://thehill.com/homenews/administration/248387-obamas-five-big-arguments-on-iran-deal. Accessed April 26, 2020.

122   F. TOUZANI

being able to provide a reasonable alternative.[147] On July 23, Obama met some unconvinced Democratic members of Congress to convince them to support the agreement.[148] On August 5, Obama delivered a speech in which he compared supporting or opposing the deal to the choice between diplomacy and war. He stated:

> The choice we face is ultimately between diplomacy and some form of war—maybe not tomorrow, maybe not three months from now, but soon. How can we in good conscience justify war before we've tested a diplomatic agreement that achieves our objectives?[149]

Obama's officials made its own lobbying endeavors. They invited the Jewish lawmakers to the White House two days after the conclusion of the deal to brief them about it and urge them to back it up.[150] Obama was trying to lobby AIPAC's first points of contact.

Finally, a resolution of disapproval on the agreement failed to pass in the Senate and so did a resolution of approval in the House.[151] Consequently, the agreement came into force after the elapse of the sixty-day congressional review period.

In brief, the humiliating defeat of AIPAC on Iran nuclear program can be attributed to two major factors. First, the Iran nuclear deal had a strong international legitimacy as it was supported by the United Nations and the International Atomic Energy Agency (IAEA). This made AIPAC's arguments against the deal weak, which resulted in harming its credibility among many members of Congress. Second, Obama was very successful

---

[147] Barack Obama, "Weekly address: A Comprehensive, Long-Term Deal with Iran," The White House, July 18, 2015, https://obamawhitehouse.archives.gov/the-press-off ice/2015/07/18/weekly-address-comprehensive-long-term-deal-iran. Accessed April 26, 2020.

[148] Jonathan Weisman and Michael Gordon, "Kerry Defends Iran Nuclear Deal Before Skeptical Senate," *The New York Times*, July 23, 2015, https://www.nytimes.com/ 2015/07/24/world/middleeast/john-kerry-defends-iran-nuclear-deal-before-skeptical-sen ate.html. Accessed April 26, 2020.

[149] Full Text: Obama Gives a Speech About the Iran Nuclear Deal, *The Washington Post*, August 5, 2015 https://www.washingtonpost.com/news/post-politics/wp/2015/ 08/05/text-obama-gives-a-speech-about-the-iran-nuclear-deal/. Accessed April 26, 2020.

[150] Note 159.

[151] Dennis Jett, *The Iran Nuclear Deal: Bombs, Bureaucrats, and Billionaires* (Springer, 2018), p. 35.

in framing the debate as a war-or-peace choice. This frame was troublesome for the public opinion taking into account the terrible effects of the war on Iraq.

All in all, it is obvious that AIPAC strives to shape foreign policy decisions in the region through various strategies. First, it targets the public opinion and tries to dominate it through monitoring the media and academia as well as ensuring a strong presence in the Washington think tanks. Second, AIPAC makes use of various strategies to gain access to members of Congress and Presidents or presidential candidates. This is accomplished through offering generous financial resources during their campaigns or via other direct means.

While we recognize the strength of AIPAC as a well-organized interest group with comprehensive lobbying strategies that enable it to have a relatively easy access to policymakers, having access to decision makers does not necessarily lead to influencing their decisions policies,

The following chapter discusses the role of another non-state actor. Namely, think tanks. In fact, some *think tanks* can also be considered interest groups, especially those which advocate for specific ideas. This type of think tanks is called "advocacy think tanks".

CHAPTER 5

Think Tanks: A Circuitous Impact on US Foreign Policy

The use of the phrase "think tank" originated during World War II. It referred to a secure place where military arrangements and strategies could be established and discussed.[1] Nowadays, defining think tanks remains problematic.

For instance, Merriam-Webster's Dictionary defines a think tank as "an institute, corporation, or group organized to study a particular subject (such as a policy issue or a scientific problem) and provide information, ideas, and advice".[2] Oxford Dictionary defines a think tank as "a body of experts providing advice and ideas on specific political or economic problems".[3]

Defining think tanks is also problematic among scholars. Many prominent scholars have given different definitions to the term "think tank". These include Abelson (2009), McGann & Weaver (2000), Smith (1991), and Stone and Denham (2004), to name a few. However, they seem to

---

[1] Stella Ladi, *Globalization, Policy Transfer and Policy Research institutes* (Edward Elgar Publishing, 2005), p. 44.

[2] *Merriam-Webster's Dictionary*, "Think tank," https://www.merriam-webster.com/dictionary/think%20tank. Accessed February 10, 2019.

[3] *Oxford Dictionaries*, s.v. "Think tank," https://en.oxforddictionaries.com/definition/think_tank. Accessed February 10, 2019.

© The Author(s), under exclusive license to Springer Nature Switzerland AG 2024
F. Touzani, *Marketing US Foreign Policy in the MENA Region*, Political Campaigning and Communication, https://doi.org/10.1007/978-3-031-45143-0_5

125

agree on their nature and function as independent and non-profit organizations that aim at affecting policies through producing and spreading scholarly research in conferences, seminars, books, papers, reports, and journals.

The role of think tanks in the US remains more important than those in Europe due to several factors. The most significant factor is party discipline. While the executive and legislative representatives of political parties in Europe tend to respect the policy advice provided by their political parties, American Presidents and members of Congress are not obliged to conform to their parties' policy commands.[4] Therefore, they are more likely to seek the expertise of think tanks to help them make domestic and foreign policies.

In fact, there have been many American policy makers, from the executive and legislative branches, who have appointed think tanks experts to work in highly ranked positions in their governments or offices. This chapter discusses the impact of US think tanks on US Presidents' foreign policies in the Middle East and North Africa in the light of three case studies: Bill Clinton (1993–2001), George Bush (2001–2009), and Barrack Obama (2009–2017). Before we get to the analysis of these case studies, it is important to examine the typologies of think tanks in the US, which helps us understand how can think tanks influence policies.

The Typologies of Think Tanks in the US

To begin with, it is important to point out that size has not been mentioned as an important defining characteristic of think tanks among scholars. This is because think tanks can range from one or two staff members to several hundreds. According to Abelson, think tanks differ in their "specialization, research output and ideological orientation, and greatly in terms of their institutional independence".[5] He distinguishes between five types of think tanks. Namely, Universities without Students, Government Contractors, Advocacy Think Tanks, Legacy-Based Think Tanks, and Policy Clubs.[6] Similarly, McGann and Weaver have identified

---

[4] Diane Stone, "Introduction: Think Tanks, Policy Advice and Governance," in Diane Stone and Andrew Denham (Eds.): *Think Tanks Traditions, Policy Research, and Politics of Ideas* (Manchester University Press, 2004), pp. 1–16 (pp. 1–2).

[5] Ibid., p.8.

[6] Ibid.

5 THINK TANKS: A CIRCUITOUS IMPACT ON US FOREIGN ... 127

four types of think tanks: Academic, or what Abelson referred to as "universities without students", Contract Researchers, Advocacy Tanks, and Party Think Tanks.[7]

A close look at the definition of each type reveals that what McGann and Weaver called "Party Think Tank" share almost the same characteristics with Abelson's "Legacy-Based Think Tanks" and "Policy Clubs". That is to say, their staff are all former or current members of a political party and their work reflects that of the party's orientation.[8] Therefore, the typology of think tanks can boil down to three major categories about which there is a consensus in the literature. Below is a brief definition of each type with its particular characteristics.

Universities Without Students/Academic Think Tanks

The staff of these think tanks are usually well-known and prolific academicians or researchers. They are called universities because their function is, first and foremost, to foster a better understanding of significant political, economic, and social issues that encounter society. In fact, this is the major mission of all regular universities.[9] However, the academicians of academic think tanks do not teach as there are no students. An example of such think tanks includes the Brookings Institution which remains one of the most famous academic think tanks in the US.

According to Abelson, academic think tanks have the following characteristics. First, they tend to focus on long and medium-term research projects which aim at examining issues that might be considered by policy makers in the future. The findings of such research projects are published in lengthy books. Second, academic think tanks are often described as independent organizations whose research standards are strictly objective. Their funding comes from various foundations, corporations, and individuals. As for their agenda, it is usually set internally by their staff.[10] Nevertheless, the level of independence of these think tanks as well as

---

[7] James G. McGann and Kent R. Weaver (Eds.), *Think Tanks and Civil Societies: Catalysts for Ideas and Action* (London: Transaction Publishers, 2000).

[8] Ibid.

[9] Donald E. Abelson, *Do Think Tanks Matter? Assessing the Impact of Public Policy Institutes*, 2nd ed. (McGill-Queen's University Press, 2009), p. 18.

[10] McGann & Weaver, *Think Tanks and Civil Societies*, p. 7.

128   F. TOUZANI

the objectivity of their research often clash with their main mission to influence policies.

Contract Think Tanks

Contract think tanks share some characteristics with the academic ones and differ in others. They both employ strong academicians and endeavor to keep objectivity and credibility as the main characteristic of their research. However, contract think tanks differ from the academic ones in their sources of funding, their main client, how they set the agenda, and the type of research they produce.

Contract think tanks usually receive funding from government agencies; these agencies play an important role in setting the agenda which should be carried out by contract think tanks. The fact that the agenda is mostly set by the funders, who are mostly policy makers, might put the objectivity and credibility of their research in question, especially if the funders try to put pressure on their contractors to alter the research findings or prevent them from being published in case they are not in line with the funders' policy convictions.

Furthermore, contract think tanks present their research findings to their funders in the form of reports rather than books or articles that are publicly circulated. Government agencies may choose to make the research outcomes publicly available. RAND and the Urban Institute are examples of contract think tanks.

Advocacy Think Tanks

These think tanks aim at informing policymakers about current critical issues. They are interested in selling their ideas to specific targets rather than striving to maintain objectivity in their research as it is the case with academic and contract think tanks. That is why their research is often characterized as "less objective and balanced".[11]

Unlike academic and contract think tanks, which aim at influencing future policies, advocacy think tanks focus on influencing current policy debates through providing policymakers and the media with very short studies in the form of one or two-page briefing notes. Additionally, most

---

[11] Abelson, *Do Think Tanks Matter?* p. 21.

5 THINK TANKS: A CIRCUITOUS IMPACT ON US FOREIGN ... 129

advocacy think tanks recruit young individuals who hold masters or PhD degrees in addition to experienced practitioners in business, government, and on Capitol Hill. Thus, the staff of advocacy think tanks tend to have a little or no experience in research.

Advocacy think tanks raise their funds mainly from their members who provide individual contributions. However, they also receive some contributions from corporations and foundations. This has enabled advocacy think tanks to market themselves as independent organizations as they mainly rely on self-funding. Another characteristic of advocacy think tanks is their use of the media to influence policymakers and the public opinion.

Table 5.1. sums up the main characteristics of academic, contract, and advocacy thinks in terms of their sources of funding, who set their agenda, their staff, their research focus, how they present their research as well as their ideological convictions.

A close look at the characteristics of the three types of think tanks in the US reveals two important facts. First, they can influence policies through the research they publish or the ideas they market. Second, none

Table 5.1 Similarities and differences between different types of US think tanks

Characteristics	Academic	Contract	Advocacy
Source of funding	Grants, endowments, corporations, and individuals	Government agencies	Mainly members but also foundations and corporations
Who set the agenda?	Staff/researchers	Government needs	Ideology
Staff	Highly experienced academicians	Highly experienced academicians	Inexperienced young researchers and experienced practitioners from different sectors
Research focus	Long and medium-term projects aiming at influencing future policies	Long and medium-term projects aiming at influencing future policies	Market their ideas to influence current policies
How is research presented?	Lengthy books and articles	Reports	Short one-to-two briefing notes and the media
Ideology	Strive to be neutral	Strive to be neutral	Liberal/ conservative

130   F. TOUZANI

of the types can claim a perfect independence because not all of them are 100% neutral, some of them have a certain level of restrictions on agenda setting and none of them are 100% self-funded.

However, we can say that while academic think tanks are the closest to being independent and neutral, contract think tanks can be positioned in the middle of the continuum and advocacy think tanks are more considered lobby groups than think tanks because their major goal is not to conduct research but to win the "war of ideas". There are similar types of think tanks, often called "party think tanks", which collect published research to support their party's positions on various issues.

THE IMPACT OF US THINK TANKS ON US FOREIGN POLICY IN THE MENA REGION: CASE STUDIES

William J. Clinton (1993–2001) and the Shift in US Foreign Policy: A Significant But Ambivalent Impact of Think Tanks

Clinton's Staff and the World of Think Tanks: A Significant Recruitment

The Clinton Administration was first associated with the Progressive Policy Institute (PPI). This think tank was established to be affiliated with the Democratic Leadership Council (DLC) of which Clinton had been the chair before he was elected the 42nd US President.[12]

According to James McGann, the "PPI serves as the research arm of the Democratic Leadership Council, a centrist democratic group that provided the intellectual and policy framework for the Clinton campaign and later the 'Clinton Agenda".[13] As a President elect, Clinton tried to apply the PPI's policy recommendations as they were outlined in its "Mandate for Change".[14] In fact, there were many strong similarities between the PPI's Mandate for Change and Clinton's first State of the

---

[12] The US Democratic Party founded the DLC in 1985 in order to alter the leftist policies it took in the late 1960s, 1970s, and the 1980s and take back the white middle class voters through designing policies that meet their needs.

[13] James G. McGann, *Think Tanks and Policy Advice in the United States: Academics, Advisors and Advocates* (Abingdon, UK: Routledge, 2007), p. 18.

[14] Donald E. Abelson, *A Capitol Idea: Think Tanks & Foreign Policy* (Quebec, Canada: McGill Queen's University Press, 2006), p. 38.

5 THINK TANKS: A CIRCUITOUS IMPACT ON US FOREIGN ... 131

Union Address.[15] However, most of the mandate's policy recommendations revolved around domestic issues such as welfare reform. This is explained by the fact that all of the PPI's staff who joined the Clinton's administration worked in the domestic policy departments. Namely, Al From, William Galston, Elaine Kamarck, and Bruce Reed.

As far as foreign policy is concerned, Clinton sought the expertise of staff from other think tanks. The most famous was Madeline Albright who was the President of the Center for National Policy (CNP) from 1989 to 1992 before joining the Clinton Administration as the US Ambassador to the United Nations (1993–1997) and, later, the Secretary of State (1997–2001). Since 2001, Ms. Albright has re-joined the world of think thinks as the Director Emerita of the Council on Foreign Relations (CFR) until she passed away in 2022.

The second prominent personality who joined Clinton's administration from think tanks was Anthony Lake. Lake served as a Foreign Service Officer in the State Department for eight years before joining the Clinton Administration. He served as one of the chief foreign policy advisers and the National Security Advisor from 1993 to 1997. Before joining the Clinton Administration, the Council on Foreign Relations (CFR) singled out Lake to conduct an analytical study on the impacts of US foreign policy in Vietnam on the American society.[16]

Before joining the Clinton Administration as the US Ambassador to the NATO from 1993 to 1998, Robert Hunter had been affiliated with the Center for Strategic and International Studies (CSIS) from 1981 to 1993. He also served in the National Security Council (NSC) during Carter's presidency. After finishing his government service, he has worked as a senior advisor at RAND Corporation.

These examples illustrate the fact that Clinton sought the expertise of think tanks' staff to serve in key foreign policy positions. These include the State Department, the United Nations, the NATO, and the NSC.

---

[15] Abelson, *Do Think Tanks Matter?* p. 189.

Bill Clinton, "State of the Union Address," Speech, The American Presidency Project, University of California Santa Barbara, Address Before a Joint Session of Congress on Administration Goals, February 17, 1993, http://www.presidency.ucsb.edu/ws/index.php?pid=47232. Accessed February 18, 2019.

[16] Anthony Lake, *The Vietnam Legacy: The War, American Society and the Future of American Foreign Policy* (New York: New York University Press, 1976).

132 F. TOUZANI

Another example, which illustrates a reverse phenomenon, is Strobe Talbott who was not part of the think tank circle before joining the Clinton Administration as Madeleine Albright's Deputy Secretary of State. Talbott joined the think tank community after finishing his government service and served as the President of Brookings Institution from 2002 to 2017.[17]

Clinton's Staff and the Types of Think Tanks They Come From:
A Balanced Combination
We notice that Clinton resorted to different types of think tanks to recruit his foreign policy staff. The Center for National Policy, now called the Truman Center for National Policy, is considered an advocacy think tank because it was founded by the former liberal cabinet members. Besides, it was mainly funded by left-wing foundations such as MacArthur Foundation, Carnegie Corporation of New York, and The Open Society Foundations, to advocate for liberal and progressive values.[18]

RAND Corporation and CSIS are generally considered contract think tanks because their main sources of funding come from contracts with government agencies and departments. Moreover, they mostly present their research in reports and articles.[19] As for the Council on Foreign Relations (CFR), it is considered an academic think tank due to the fact that it is funded by diverse sources which do not include government contracts. Rather, they include individuals, corporate memberships, revenues from *Foreign Affairs* magazine in addition to donations from foundations and endowments.[20] Additionally, the CFR produces its research in different forms including lengthy books. RAND, CSIS, and CFR are all known for their independent research and strive for neutrality.

[17] Strobe Talbott is currently a distinguished fellow in residence in the Foreign Policy program at the Brookings Institution, https://www.brookings.edu/experts/strobe-talbott/. Accessed March 20, 2019.

[18] More information on the Center for National Policy can be found in the website of Influence Watch Organization. https://www.influencewatch.org/non-profit/center-for-national-policy/. Accessed April 16, 2019.

[19] The information about RAND and CSIS were retrieved from their websites respectively. https://www.rand.org/about/glance.html and https://www.csis.org/programs/about-us. Accessed April 17, 2019.

[20] Council on Foreign Relation, about CFR: Funding, https://www.cfr.org/funding. Accessed February 4, 2019.

5 THINK TANKS: A CIRCUITOUS IMPACT ON US FOREIGN ... 133

Clinton's Policies in the MENA Region: From "Assertive Multilateralism" to a Unilateral Approach

The fact that all of Clinton's key foreign policy staff came from independent or progressive think tanks may explain Clinton's foreign policy strategy of "assertive multilateralism" which was credited to Madeline Albright. The principle of "assertive multilateralism" focuses on multilateral cooperation to reduce military expenditure and human losses associated with US international military participation.[21]

This foreign policy strategy was adopted in the first-half of Clinton's first term through endorsing the United Nations Security Council Resolutions 661 and 687 against Iraq. The resolutions involve imposing economic sanctions on this country, applying no-fly zones, and inspecting Iraq's potential acquisition of weapons of mass destruction.[22] However, the assertive multilateralism tactic diminished after the 1994 US elections which was a turning point in Clinton's foreign policy in general, especially in the Middle East.

The 1994 US elections, which were held in the middle of Clinton's first term, was known as the Republican Revolution because Republicans won sweeping majorities in both the House and the Senate as well as governorship. This marked the end of the Democratic control for the first time in 40 years and allowed Republicans to maintain their control of both the House and the Senate for the remaining six years of Clinton's tenure.[23]

Such a drastic change coincided with a harsh criticism of Clinton's foreign policy including the one in the Middle East. The criticism came mainly from conservative think tanks such as Heritage Foundation and

---

[21] Jennifer Sterling-Folker, "Between a Rock and a Hard Place: Assertive and Post Cold-War US Foreign Policy," In James M. Scott (Ed.): *After the End: Making US Foreign Policy in the Post-Cold-War World* (Durham: Duke University Press, 1998), pp. 277–304.

[22] United Nations Security Council Resolution 661, Iraq-Kuwait, August 6, 1990, http://unscr.com/en/resolutions/661 and United Nations Security Council Resolution 687, Iraq-Kuwait, April 3, 1991, http://unscr.com/en/resolutions/687.

[23] Adam Clymer, "The 1994 Elections: Congress, the Overview; G.O.P celebrates its sweep to Power; Clinton Vows to Find Common Ground," *New York Times*, November 10, 1994, https://www.nytimes.com/1994/11/10/us/1994-elections-con gress-overview-gop-celebrates-its-sweep-power-clinton-vows.html. Accessed February 20, 2019.

134   F. TOUZANI

American Enterprise Institute (AEI).[24] The criticism was intensified with the establishment of a fledgling neoconservative think tank in 1997. Namely, the Project for the New American Century (PNAC).

PNAC's Statement of Principles described the US as the "world's preeminent power" which encounters a challenge to "shape a new century favorable to American principles and interests" through advocating for an "increase in defense spending" and "challenge regimes hostile to our interests and values".[25] By hostile regimes, PNAC was referring to, first and foremost, Saddam Hussein's Iraq. PNAC increased its criticism of Clinton's foreign policy in this country, especially during his second term.

The criticism culminated in drafting an open letter from PNAC to President Clinton on January 26, 1998. The letter asked Clinton to seek the "removal of Saddam Hussein's regime from power".[26] It was signed by prominent conservatives and former officials of Republican administrations many of whom would later serve in key positions in the Bush administration. These include Donald Rumsfeld, Richard Armitage, Paul Wolfowitz, Elliott Abrams, John Bolton, Paula Dobriansky, and Robert Zoellick.

In addition to PNAC, Abelson noted that from 1998 to 2008, the Heritage Foundation, along with conservative members of the AEI, CSIS, Cato, and RAND, were more often invited to provide testimonies before the Republican-controlled Congress than the Brookings Institution which is generally known for its liberal views.[27]

The Republican pressure from Congress combined with the harsh criticism from conservative think tanks forced Clinton to abandon his "assertive multilateralism". Instead, he adopts foreign policies characterized by a raise in defense expenditure, a decrease in US engagements in international organizations, a dedication to enlarging the NATO, and a

---

[24] David D. Newsom, *The Public Dimension of Foreign* (Bloomington, IN: Indiana University Press), 147.

[25] The Project for New American Century, Statement of Principles, June 3, 1997, https://www.rrojasdatabank.info/pfpc/PNAC---statement%20of%20principles.pdf.

[26] Project for the New American Century, Letter to President Clinton, January 26, 1998, https://web.archive.org/web/20130112203258/http://www.newamericanc entury.org/iraqclintonlet ter.html. Accessed February 22, 2019.

[27] Abelson, *Do Think Think Tanks Matter?* pp. 174–176.

strong policy aiming at imposing more sanctions on Iraq and other hostile nations in the region such as Iran, Lybia, and the Sudan.[28]

Since 1996, Clinton adopted a unilateral diplomatic and military approach which focuses on imposing more sanctions on Iraq and tracing Osama Bin Laden in the Sudan and Afghanistan. To illustrate, Clinton ordered the Operation Desert Strike in September 1996 against Iraqi Air Defense in response to Saddam Hussein's attempt to attack Iraqi Kurdistan. On October 31, 1998, Clinton signed the Iraq Liberation Act which aimed at removing Saddam Hussein from power.[29] This law was implemented between December 16 and 19, 1998 through launching concentrated air strikes against military installations in Iraq claiming that Hussein had not cooperated with the UN inspectors for weapons of mass destructions.

Clinton continued his deviation from "assertive multilateralism" through signing two executive orders against Iran: 12,957 and 12,959. These executive orders aimed at imposing more oil sanctions on this country. They also banned American companies and their foreign subsidiaries from engaging in any kind of oil trade relations with it claiming that it is a "state sponsor of terrorism" and a "rogue state".[30]

Clinton continued his unilateral foreign policy in the Middle East to track Osama Bin Laden in Afghanistan and the Sudan. On August 20, 1998, he ordered a cruise missile strikes on Al Qaeda training camps in Afghanistan and a pharmaceutical factory in the Sudan. The Sudan was suspected for hosting Bin Laden and producing biological weapons. However, these attacks failed to capture or kill Bin Laden.

To recapitulate, the Clinton's case study shows that think tanks might have played an important role in shaping his foreign policy in the MENA

---

[28] James D. Boys, "A Lost Opportunity: The Flawed Implementation of Assertive Multilateralism (1991–1993)," European Journal of American studies [Online], 7–1 | 2012, document 6, Online since December 17, 2012, http://journals.openedition.org/ejas/9924. Accessed February 26, 2019.

[29] H.R.4655—Iraq Liberation Act of 1998, October 31, 1998, https://www.congress.gov/bill/105th-congress/house-bill/4655. Accessed February 26, 2019.

[30] William J. Clinton, Executive Order 12,957, "Prohibiting Certain Transactions With Respect to the Development of Iranian Petroleum Resources," March 15, 1995, https://en.m.wikisource.org/wiki/Executive_Order_12957.

William J. Clinton, Executive Order 12,959. "Prohibiting Certain Transactions With Respect to Iran," May 6, 1995, https://en.m.wikisource.org/wiki/Executive_Order_12959#/search. Accessed February 26, 2019.

136   F. TOUZANI

area. To begin with, all of his prominent foreign policy personnel were recruited from a combination of academic, contract, and advocacy think tanks. Most of these think tanks are known for their independent or liberal views. These include Madeline Albright whose Assertive Multilateralism did not prevail long and was confronted with the rise of conservative think tanks, especially after the 1994 elections which resulted in a strong control of Congress by Republicans.

The Clinton's case study does not suggest that the shift in Clinton's foreign policy was causatively related to the pressure from conservative think tanks. Rather, this case presents some strong indicators which illustrate the influence that conservative think tanks could have had on Clinton's foreign policy in the Middle East. These indicators include the shift in Clinton's foreign policy in the region after the harsh criticism from conservative think tanks, especially PNAC. This coincided with a sweeping Republican control of Congress. The shift in Clinton's foreign policy was illustrated by the examples we provided on Iraq, Iran, and Osama Bin Laden. Another indicator is Abelson's finding that conservative think tanks were dominantly invited to provide testimonies in Congress after Republicans took over the legislative power during Clinton's presidency.

George W. Bush (2001–2009): A Circuitous Impact of Conservative Think Tanks

The Bush Staff and Their Affiliations with Think Tanks:
A Conservative Dominance
The potential influence of think tanks on Bush's foreign policy started during his presidential campaign in 2000 when he reunited a team of friends and policy advisers. As a matter of fact, most of those friends and advisors were affiliated with conservative think tanks such as the Hoover Institution, the American Enterprise Institute (AEI), and the newly established Project for New American Century (PNAC).[31] These "Vulcans",

---

[31] Abelson, *Do Think Think Tanks Matter?* 144.

5 THINK TANKS: A CIRCUITOUS IMPACT ON US FOREIGN ...   137

as some prefer to call them, had already served in previous Republican administrations before joining the Bush Administration.[32] The most prominent among those were Dick Cheney and Donald Rumsfeld.

Dick Cheney, who was Bush's Vice President during his two terms (2001–2009), was affiliated with the AEI and so was his wife, Lynne. Dick Cheney frequently mentioned the AEI in his memoirs more than any other think tank. After finishing his service with Bush senior's government, in which he served as Secretary of Defense from 1989 to 1993, he joined the AEI to "continue to contribute on the major policy and political debates of the day".[33] In the acknowledgment of the same book, Cheney stated "I'd like to thank the American Enterprise Institute, with which I've been long associated, and its outstanding and visionary president Arthur Brooks for the many forums the organization has provided over the years for debate about the most important policy issues of our time".[34]

Before serving as Secretary of Defense in Bush junior Administration from 2001 to 2006, Donald Rumsfeld served in the same position in President Gerald Ford administration (1975–1977) and US Ambassador to the NATO (1973–1974). Rumsfeld was associated with various think tanks most of which are considered conservative. These include the Center for Security Policy (CSP), the Hoover Institution, the Project for New American Century (PNAC), and RAND Corporation.

The fact that George W. Bush relied on these prominent individuals in his administration cannot be explained by their affiliation with the think tanks we mentioned. Rather, George W. Bush singled them out because of their political experience serving in previous Republican administrations including his father's. In fact, both Cheney and Rumsfeld were recruited by think thanks because of their political experience serving in previous administrations not because of their academic or scholarly abilities.

The two most powerful men in Bush administration, Cheney and Rumsfeld, were signatories of PNAC's founding Statement of Principles. This statement had been drafted before Bush came into power in 2001. In fact, 10 of the 25 signatories of this statement joined the Bush

---

[32] James Mann, *The Rise of the Vulcans: The History of Bush's War Cabinet* (New York, NY: Penguin Group, 2004), p. XV.

[33] Richard. B. Cheney, *In My Time: A Personal and Political Memoir* (New York, NY: Threshold Editions, 2011), p. 241.

[34] Ibid., 521.

138   F. TOUZANI

administration afterward. In addition to Cheney and Rumsfeld, there were:

- Paul Wolfowitz, Deputy Secretary of Defense.
- Eliot A. Cohen, a Counselor of the State Department and member of the Committee for the Liberation of Iraq.
- Paula Dobriansky, under Secretary of State for Democracy and Global Affairs.
- Zalmay Khalilzad, US ambassador to the UN, Iraq, and Afghanistan.
- Scooter Libby, chief of Staff to Vice President Dick Cheney.
- Elliot Abrams, senior member of the National Security Council.
- Aaron Friedberg, vice President's Deputy National Security Advisor and the Vice President's Director of Policy Planning.
- Fred Ikle, member of the Defense Policy Board.

Bush's Policies in the MENA Region: A Reflection of PNAC's Policy Recommendations
In 2000, PNAC has conducted a major study: "Rebuilding America's Defenses". The study provided a clear recommendation on Iraq: "While the unresolved conflict with Iraq provides the immediate justification, the need for a substantial American force presence in the Gulf transcends the issue of the regime of Saddam Hussein".[35]

It is very important to note that PNAC's study was conducted before 9/11 and few months before Bush came to power with a government that constituted of 40% of PNAC's Statement of Principles signatories. To put it differently, it was not only due to 9/11 or Saddam Hussein's regime that George W. Bush decided to invade Iraq, but it was also because Bush key staff from PNAC had already been convinced of the necessity to maintain a strong US military presence in the Middle East. Indeed, PNAC's heavy criticism of Clinton's foreign policy in the Middle East was replaced by an unambiguous boost of Bush policy in the region.

The lamentable events of 9/11 provided a certain level of credibility to neoconservative think tanks, especially PNAC with its impactful

---

[35] The Project for the New American Century, *Rebuilding America's Defenses: Strategy, Forces and Resources for a New Century* (September 2000), 14. Accessed on March 1, 2019, https://web.archive.org/web/20130112234519/http://newamericancentury. org/RebuildingAmerica sDefenses.pdf.

5 THINK TANKS: A CIRCUITOUS IMPACT ON US FOREIGN ... 139

connections with Republican officials. In his analysis of a wide spectrum of commentators, Donald Abelson concluded that PNAC's policies and principles, which were considered by the majority as extreme and disagreeable before 9/11, became more appealing afterward.[36]

Few days after 9/11, PNAC sent a letter to George W. Bush to present its vision about the war on terror. This letter highlighted some recommendations such as pursuing military operations in Iraq and Afghanistan to topple Saddam Hussein and capture or kill Osama Bin Laden, This is in addition to insulating Hezbollah, stopping financial support to the Palestinian Authority, and increasing defense spending to accomplish all these goals.[37] Interestingly enough, the letter did not mention anything about Iran and North Korea and the threats their ballistic missile programs might pose to the security of the US.

The strong alinement between PNAC's recommendations and the vision of Bush's foreign policy in the Middle East is more than a coincidence taking into consideration the strong connections that this neoconservative think tank had with Bush's inner circle. Bush's adoption of PNAC'x foreign policy recommendations about the MENA region is not to be attributed to the importance of PNAC as a think tank which is supposed to provide independent and objective policy recommendations. In fact, the strong alignment is mostly attributed to those prominent Republican politicians who founded PNAC and whose neoconservative policy convictions preceded its birth.

Bush never mentioned PNAC's role in providing him with policy recommendations. however, he frequently mentioned Cheney and Rumsfeld for the same purpose. A further point that supports this conclusion is the fact that PNAC's prominence gradually faded away after most of its prominent founders joined the Bush administration until it ceased its function in 2006. Thus, we can consider PNAC an anomaly when we analyze the strong connections between its policy recommendations and Bush's foreign policy vision in the MENA region.

---

[36] Donald Abelson, *A Capitol Idea*, 212.

[37] Project for the New American Century, Letter to President Bush, September 20, 2001. Archived website, accessed March 9, 2019. https://web.archive.org/web/201301 12203258/ http://www.newamericancentury.org/.

140   F. TOUZANI

Bush War on Terror: Different Recommendations from Different Think Tanks

The option of going to war was shared by other conservative think tanks including AEI, Heritage Foundation, and the Hoover Institute. On the other hand, other major think tanks had balanced views in this regard. For example, the Carnegie Endowment for International Peace (CEIP) was antiwar and recommended other non-military ways to deal with potential WMDs acquisition by Iraq.[38]

While some scholars from Brookings were in favor of invading Iraq and overthrowing Saddam Hussein, others suggested more discussion in Congress. The Council on Foreign Relations (CFR) was against using force to contain or disarm Saddam Hussein's regime. The same argument was shared by Cato Institute which taught that Iraq did not threaten US security. There were also some prominent think tanks which preferred to give no recommendations about going to war in Iraq such as CSIS.[39]

Bush and Pro-Israel Think Tanks: A Significant Recruitment

Another very important aspect of Bush's foreign policy in the Middle East in relation to US think tanks was the "Israeli Lobby". A pertinent study conducted by John Mearsheimer and Stephen M. Walt concluded that the number of connections between some of Bush leading pro-Israel staff and pro-Israel think tanks was abundant, especially with PNAC, AEI, CSP, Hudson Institute, the Jewish Institute for National Security of America (JINSA), the Middle East Forum, and the Washington Institute for Near East Policy.[40] These leading personnel included the following:

> Elliott Abrams was born into a Jewish family. He served as a special assistant to President Bush as well as the National Security Council's senior director for Near East and North African Affairs. Abrams was a co-founder of PNAC and CSP which were both known for their strong support for Israel.

---

[38] Ellen Laipson, "Think Tanks: Supporting Cast Players in the National Security Enterprise," in G. Roger and Harry Rishikof (Eds.): *The National Security Enterprise: Navigating the Labyrinth* (Washington, DC: Georgetown University Press), pp. 289–299.

[39] Ibid.

[40] John, J, Mearsheimer and Stephen M. Walt, *The Israel Lobby and U.S. Foreign Policy* (New York, NY: Farrar, Straus and Giroux, 2007), pp. 129–131.

5 THINK TANKS: A CIRCUITOUS IMPACT ON US FOREIGN ... 141

John Bolton served as the Under Secretary of State for Arms Control and International Security (2001–2005) and US ambassador to the United Nations (2005–2006) during Bush Administration. Before joining the Bush Administration, Bolton was a senior Vice President at the AEI. The AEI was one of those conservative think tanks which are known for their strong support for Israel. After completing his service with the Bush Administration, Bolton served as the chairman of the Gatestone Institute from 2013 to 2018. The Gatestone Institute is a conservative think tank which was criticized for spreading untrue anti-Muslim information.[41] Bolton was behind the three-state solution to the Palestinian-Israeli conflict. He suggested returning the control of Gaza to Egypt and the West Bank to Jordan.[42] Such a clearly biased solution, which would deprive the Palestinians from establishing their own state, showed the strong support that Bolton expressed for Israel. In fact, he described the Palestinian right to have their own state as a "ploy".[43] In 2010, Bolton co-founded Friends of Israel Initiative, along with 12 other prominent international personalities, to counter efforts to delegitimize the state of Israel.[44]

Born to a Jewish family, Douglas Feith is a neoconservative who served as the Under Secretary of Defense in the Bush Administration from 2001 to 2005. Feith was the director of the Center for National Security Strategies at Hudson Institute which remains an ardent pro-Israel think tank. In fact, the Gatestone Institute, which was chaired by John Bolton, started as a satellite office of the Hudson Institute in New York. Furthermore, According to Didi Ramez and Shira Beery, US and Israeli tax documents revealed that Hudson is a major

[41] Heidi Przybyla, "John Bolton Presided over Anti-Muslim Think Tank," nbcnews.com, April 23, 2018, *NBC News*, Accessed March 5, 2019. https://www.nbc news.com/politics/white-house/john-bolton-chaired-anti-muslim-think-tank-n868171.

[42] John R. Bolton, "The Three-State Solution," washingtonpost.com, January 5, 2009. *The Washington Post*, http://www.washingtonpost.com/wp-dyn/content/article/2009/01/04/AR2009010401434.html?noredirect=on. Accessed March 5, 2019.

[43] John R.Bolton "How to Block the Palestinian Statehood Ploy," wsj.com, June 3, 2011, *The Wall Street Journal*, https://www.wsj.com/articles/SB1000142405270230365 7404576357721571060778. Accessed March 5, 2019.

[44] For more information on the organization, visit their website http://www.friendsof israelinitiative.org.

financial supporter of the Institute for Zionist Strategies (IZS) with hundreds of thousands of dollars over few years.[45]

Scooter Libby, born to a Jewish family and one of the *Vulcans*, served as Cheney's chief of staff and was involved in Bush endeavors to negotiate Israeli-Palestinian Road Map for Peace through taking part in many meetings with Israeli leaders in 2002 and 2003. Libby was one of the co-founders of PNAC which was a strong pro-Israel think tank. Mearsheimer and Walt described Libby as the "most fervently pro-Israel official" in the Bush Administration.[46]

Richard Perle, the son of Jewish parents, served as the chairman of the Defense Policy Board Advisory Committee in the Bush Administration from 2001 to 2003. Perle has been involved with many conservative pro-Israel think tanks such as the Washington Institute for Near East Policy (WINEP), CSP, AEI, PNAC, and the Jewish. Institute for National Security Affairs (JINSA). Perle authored, along with David Wurmser, Douglas Feith, and others, a policy document for Benjamin Netanyahu, the then Israeli Prime Minister. The document, entitled "A Clean Break: A New Strategy for Securing the Realm", proposed a new approach to dealing with the Palestinians through holding the right to "hot pursue" them and promote alternatives to Arafat's leadership.[47]

David Wurmser, Perle's co-author of *"A Clean Break"*, served as Dick Cheney's Middle East advisor and special assistant to John Bolton. Wurmser has been involved with the AEI as a research fellow on the Middle East.

Last but not least, there is Paul Wolfowitz who was born to a Jewish family and served as the Deputy Secretary of Defense in the Bush Administration. Wolfowitz was a scholar at the AEI and one of the signatories of PNAC's Statement of Principles.

---

[45] Didi Remez, "Hudson Institute Primary Financial Backer of NGO Behind Campaign to Purge Israeli Universities of "Leftists," August 19, 2010, *Coderet*, https://didiremez. wordpress.com/2010/08/19/hudson-inst-primary-financial-backer-of-ngo-behind-cam paign-to-purge-israeli-universities-of-leftists/. Accessed March 6, 2019.

[46] Mearsheimer and Walt, The Israel Lobby, 20.

[47] "A Clean Break: A New Strategy for Securing the Realm, January 25, 2014, at the Wayback Machine, Institute for Advanced Strategic and Political Studies, July 2006.

All in all, the Bush case study suggests two major findings. First, the large number of high-ranking personnel who joined the Bush Administration from PNAC and the strong connections between this latter's policy recommendations and Bush's foreign policy vision in the MENA region cannot be attributed to PNAC as a think tank. An objective think tank is supposed to provide scholarly and independent research. Therefore, these strong connections were mainly attributed to the individuals who founded PNAC. In fact, most of these individuals were politicians, not academicians, who served in previous republican administrations and their neoconservative political convictions preceded the establishment of PNAC. Indeed, it was their political experience that encouraged Bush to recruit them to serve in his administration and adopt their neoconservative ideologies. The establishment of PNAC was just a tool to channel these already-established ideologies. The second major finding pertains to the large number of personnel who joined the Bush administration from pro-Israel think tanks.

Barack Obama (2009–2017): A Unique Case in Many Ways

Obama Staff: Think Tanks and The Obamians
The first term of Barack Obama's tenure was mainly characterized by managing what he inherited from his predecessor, especially Iraq, Afghanistan, and Osama Ben Laden. These issues were expanded in the second term to include the Arab Spring with the war in Libya, the rise of ISIS, Iran's nuclear program as well as the conflict in Syria.

To deal with these issues, Obama sought the help of what James Mann called the "Obamians" who greatly differed from Bush's "Vulcans".[48] Donald Abelson noticed that these Obamians represented a newer generation of experts and were recruited from many think tanks to establish Obama's foreign policies including the ones in the MENA area. These think tanks included a combination of an academic, contract, and advocacy think tanks. Namely, the Council on Foreign Relations (CFR), the Center for Strategic and International Studies (CSIS), the Center of American Progress (CAP), and the Washington Institute of Near East

---

[48] James Mann, *The Obamians: The Struggle Inside the White House to Redefine American Power* (New York, NY: Penguin Group, 2012).

144   F. TOUZANI

Policy (WINEP).[49] While CFR is considered an academic think tank, CSIS is categorized as a contract think tank and both CAP and WINEP belong to the advocacy category.

Obama's Policies and Think Tanks' Recommendations: A Striking Similarity

CAP was established in 2003 by John Podesta who co-chaired Obama's transition team into the presidency and served as his Counselor. CAP aimed at representing the liberal view as opposed to the AEI and the Heritage Foundation which represent the conservative view.

According to *Politico*, CAP was "a key ally of Obama White House, developing policy plans that included an outline for the withdrawal of American troops from Iraq".[50] In fact, Obama himself clearly stated "I could not be more grateful to CAP not only for giving me a lot of good policy ideas but also giving me a lot of staff".[51] Indeed, about one third of CAP's staff joined Obama administration.[52] Few months before Obama became the President, CAP, along with the New Democracy Project, had published a document of about 600 pages. The document was entitled "Change for America: A Progressive Blueprint for the 44th President".[53] This document constituted of 67 essays which examined various issues pertaining to the White House as well as domestic, economic, and national security policies.

As for the relevant policy recommendations pertaining to the MENA area, the focus was on responsibly withdrawing from Iraq, reducing America's dependence on the region's oil, closing Guantanamo Bay as well as using more diplomacy or soft power.

[49] McGann & Weaver, *Think Tanks and Civil Societies*, p. 147.

[50] Ben Smith, "Podesta to Step Down at CAP", *Politico*, November 24, 2011. https://www.politico.com/story/2011/10/podesta-to-step-down-at-cap-066742. Accessed March 24, 2019.

[51] Barack'Obama, "Remarks on the Economy," December 4, 2013, https://www.washingtonpost.com/politics/running-transcript-president-obamas-december-4-remarks-on-the-economy/2013/12/04/7cec31ba-5cff-11e3-be07-006c776266ed_story.html?noredirect=on. Accessed March 24, 2019.

[52] Tevi Troy, "The Dilemma of the DC Think Tank," *The Atlantic*, December 19, 2017, https://www.theatlantic.com/politics/archive/2017/12/presidents-and-think-tanks/548765/. Accessed March 26, 2019.

[53] Mark Green and Michele Jolin (Ed.), *Change for America: A Progressive Blueprint for the 44th President* (Basic Books, 2009).

Indeed, the last US troops withdrew from Iraq on November 18, 2011, before they came back in 2014 with the rise of ISIL. The US imports of oil from the Arab Gulf countries were down by 40% from 2008 to 2013.[54] Obama delivered a speech to talk about his plan to close Guantanamo saying that this detention facility "does not advance our (US) national security; it undermines it".[55] Last but not least, Obama's record of the use of diplomacy and soft power in the Middle East is absolutely more positive at least in comparison to his Republican predecessors, Bush and his father.

While the fact that Obama's policies in the region are in line with the recommendations highlighted in Change for America, this does not necessarily mean that there is a causal relationship between Obama's adopted policies and the two think tanks which came up with these policy recommendations. However, Obama's strong connections to CAP and his clear praise of its policy ideas and staff suggest that this think tank might have had an impact on Obama's foreign policy decision in the MENA region.

In addition to CAP, which represented the dovish wing of the Democratic view, Obama sought the expertise of other scholars from another think tank that represented the hawkish wing of the Democratic view. This think tank was the Center for New American Security (CNAS) which was established by Kurt Campbell and Michele Flournoy in 2007. These two scholars were the most prominent CNAS staff who joined Obama administration. Flournoy served as Obama's Undersecretary of Defense Policy from 2009 to 2012. As for Kurt Campbell, he occupied the position of the Undersecretary of State from 2009 to 2013.

When they joined Obama administration, CNAS was presided by Col. John Nagl who was the advisor of General David Petraeus, the commander of the military coalition in Iraq then. This explains CNAS main focus on US national security and defense policies, especially the issue of terrorism. Interestingly enough, many scholars considered CNAS

---

[54] Herman Franssen, "Obama and Declining US Dependence on Imported Oil and Gas," Middle East Institute (2014).

[55] Barack Obama, "Remarks by the President on Plan to Close the Prison at Guantanamo Bay," *The White House*, Office of the Press Secretary, February 23, 2016, http://obamawhitehouse.archives.gov/the-press-office/2016/02/23/remarks-president-plan-close-prison-Guantanamo-bay.

146   F. TOUZANI

as the Democratic version of PNAC in terms of their keenness on maintaining US military presence in the world. However, CNAS advocated for less presence, especially after the very costly war in Iraq.

Another fact explaining CNAS leaning toward maintaining military presence in the Middle East was its sources of funding. Its funds came from arms manufacturers and defense companies such as Northrop Grumman Aerospace Systems, Neal Blue, Airbus, Boeing, BAE Systems, Leonardo DRS, Huntington Ingalls Industries, Leidos, and Lockheed Martin.[56]

Before founding CNAS, Flournoy and Campbell were working with the Center for Strategic and International Studies (CSIS). While they were at CSIS, they had edited a book titled "To Prevail: An American Strategy For the Campaign Against Terrorism" two months after September 11, 2001.[57] This book supported Bush's decision to attack terrorist groups as well as the states that support them or cannot fight them on their lands.

In 2003, they, along with 13 other democratic scholars, signed the "Progressive Internationalism: A Democratic National Security Strategy". In this document, the signatories reiterated their support for the war on terror. However, they criticized the diplomatic failure of President Bush to convince all US allies and gain their trust to support him.[58] During the election campaign, Campbell and Flournoy presented their policy recommendations to the next president in a document titled "The Inheritance and the Way Forward". In this document, they stood against Bush's concept of preventive war and advocated for a redirection of the war on terror to ensure that the US would not lose its Muslim allies.[59]

In fact, we cannot say that Obama redirected the war on terror from the Middle East. However, we can argue that he expanded it to Africa. The focus on the Middle East became less intensive and less aggressive

[56] CNAS Supporters, Cash Contributions Received October 1, 2017 to September 30, 2018, https://www.cnas.org/support-cnas/cnas-supporters. Accessed March 28, 2019.

[57] Kurt Campbell and Michele Flournoy, "To Prevail: An American Strategy for the Campaign Against Terrorism," CSIS Significant Issues Series, CSIS, November 2001.

[58] "Progressive Internationalism: A Democratic National Security Strategy," Progressive Policy Institute, October 30, 2003.

[59] Kurt Campbell and Michele Flournoy, "The Intermittence and the Way Forward," Center for News American Security, 2007.

5 THINK TANKS: A CIRCUITOUS IMPACT ON US FOREIGN ... 147

in comparison to his predecessor. Obama used more diplomatic means as recommended by "The Inheritance and the Way Forward".[60] Obama's speech "A New Beginning", which he delivered in Egypt few months after joining the White House, was meant to rebuild US relations with the Muslim world after being critically damaged during Bush presidency. Indeed, rebuilding US relations with the Muslim world was one of the recommendations of CNAS aforementioned policy document.[61]

In addition to these two advocacy think tanks, there were other types which provided Obama with experts in foreign and defense policies. These included Susan Rice who had worked with Brookings, an academic think tank, before joining Obama's presidential campaign as his senior foreign policy advisor and Ambassador to the UN during Obama's first term.[62] From 2013 to 2017, Susan Rice served as the National Security Advisor. She strongly supported a military intervention to topple Muaamar Gaddafi in Libya.[63] In March 2011 and after an initial reluctance, Obama authorized air attacks on Lybia to enforce the UNSC Resolution 1973 and create a no-fly zone. This action was advocated for by Susan Rice who was the US Ambassador to the UN.[64] In 2012, Rice denounced the Russian and Chinese veto to a UN Security Council Resolution calling Bashar Al-Assad to step down from governing Syria.[65]

[60] Ibid.

[61] Barack Obama, "A New Beginning," Cairo, Egypt, June 4, 2009, https://obamaw hitehouse.archives.gov/issues/foreign-policy/presidents-speech-cairo-a-new-beginning.

[62] The Brookings is considered an academic think tank because it relies on different sources of funding that exclude US government funding in addition to the fact it presents its research in books and academic journals. https://www.brookings.edu/about-us/.

[63] Gerald Helguero, "US Supports Libya No-Fly Zone, Seeks Broader Action," International Business Times, March 17, 2011 https://archive.is/20120715063810/ http://uk.ibtimes.com/articles/124009/20110317/libya-no-fly-zone-hillary-clinton-uni ted-nations-susan-rice.htm. Accessed March 28, 2019.

[64] United Nations Security Council Resolution S/RES/1973, The Security Council, March 17, 2011, https://www.securitycouncilreport.org/un-documents/document/ Libya-S-RES-1973.php.

[65] Alicia Cohen, "Amb. Rice Says Russia, China, Will "Come to Regret" Vetoing UN Syria Resolution," The Hill, February 6, 2012, https://thehill.com/video/administr ation/208773-susan-rice-condemns-russia-and-china-for-voting-with-syrias-assad. Accessed March 28, 2019.

148 F. TOUZANI

Obama also insisted that Al-Assad "must go" in an address to the UN General Assembly.[66]

Furthermore, Susan Rice was often criticized for her combative tone against Israel. As a result, it contributed in intensifying the provisional tension between Israel and Obama, especially after Israeli Prime Minister Netanyahu's speech in which he harshly criticized Obama's nuclear deal with Iran.[67] Obama's relationship with Israel was characterized by tension, especially after his nuclear deal with Iran and the US abstention from vetoing a UNSC resolution which calls Israel to immediately stop its settlement activities in the West Bank and East Jerusalem.[68] The US abstention allowed the resolution to pass, which was the first time the US did not use its veto against an anti-Israel UN resolution.

Chuck Hagel was the President of the Atlantic Council before joining the Obama Administration as Secretary of Defense from 2013 to 2015. After this experience, he returned to the Atlantic Council.[69] Obama's choice of Hagel remains interesting because it is one of very few cases when a Democratic President chooses a Republican to serve in his administration as Hagel was a Republican Senator of Nebraska from 1997 to 2009. This might be explained by Hagel's foreign policy views in the Middle East as he was his party's most outspoken critic of Bush's foreign policy in the region.

Hagel once stated: "There will not be a military solution to Iraq. Iraq belongs to the 25 million Iraqis who live there. It doesn't belong to the United States. Iraq is not a prize to be won or lost".[70] In December 2005, Hagel addressed Bush and the Republican Party saying: "I took an oath of office to the Constitution, I didn't take an oath of office to my

---

[66] Barack Obama, "Address to the United Nations General Assembly," New York, September 28, 2015, http://responsibilitytoprotect.org/US_en_0.pdf. Accessed March 28, 2019.

[67] Dennis Ross, *Doomed to Succeed: The US-Israel Relationship from Truman to Obama* (McMillan, 2015), p. 366.

[68] UN Security Council Resolution 2334, December 23, 2016, https://www.un.org/webcast/pdfs/SRES2334-2016.pdf.

[69] The Atlantic Council is considered an academic think tank because it relies on different sources of funding that excludes US government funding in addition to the fact it presents its research in books and academic journals.

[70] Jeff Zeleny and Carl Hulse, "Senate Supports a Pullout Date in Iraq War Bill," *New York Times*, March 27, 2007, https://www.nytimes.com/2007/03/28/washington/28cong.html. Accessed April 5, 2019.

5 THINK TANKS: A CIRCUITOUS IMPACT ON US FOREIGN ...   149

party or my President".[71] In July 2006, Hagel criticized the way Bush reacted to the 2006 Lebanon War between Israel and Hezbollah stating: "The sickening slaughter on both sides must end and it must end now. President Bush must call for an immediate ceasefire. This madness must stop". He also said "Our relationship with Israel is special and historic... But it need not and cannot be at the expense of our Arab and Muslim relationships. That is an irresponsible and dangerous false choice".[72]

However, as the Secretary of Defense, Hagel maintained a strong relationship with Israel's Minister of Defense, Moshe Ya'alon. Ya'alon called Hagel a "true friend".[73] Despite the fact that Hagel's relationship with the White House impaired, which led to his resignation in 2015, Hagel had an excellent relationship with Israeli military officials. This was in stark contrast to how he was viewed before he was appointed the Secretary of Defense.[74]

In July 2007, he was one of only three Republican Senators who voted in favor of an Obama-sponsored bill that calls for the withdrawal of US troops from Iraq by March 31, 2008.[75] In 2008, accompanied by Obama, then a Senator, and Jack Reed, another Democratic Senator of Rhode Ireland, visited Iraq to meet US service members, General Davis Patraeus and Iraq's Prime Minister Nour Al-Maliki. Clearly, Obama's choice of Hagel was not because of this latter's affiliation with the Atlantic Council. Rather, it was mainly due to his harsh criticism of the Bush Administration and his foreign policy views in the Middle East.

To recapitulate, Obama's case study can be considered unique in many ways. First, he sought the expertise of many staff from academic, contract, and advocacy think tanks. More particularly, the advocacy think tanks,

---

[71] Charles Babington, "4 GOP Senators Hold Firm Against Patriot Act Renewal More Safeguards Needed, They Say," *The Washington Post*, December 21, 2005, http://www.washingtonpost.com/wp-dyn/content/article/2005/12/20/AR2005 122001488.html?nav=rss_print/asection&noredirect=on. Accessed April 5, 2019.

[72] "Key Republican breaks with Bush on Mideast; Nebraska's Sen. Hagel Calls for Immediate cease-fire," CNN, online edition, July 31, 2006. http://edition.cnn.com/2006/POLITICS/07/31/hagel.mideast/. Accessed April 6, 2019.

[73] Michael Wilber and Herb Keinon, "Ya'alon Praises Chuck Hagel as True Friend", November 24, 2004, *The Jerusalem Post*, https://m.jpost.com/Israel-News/Politics-And-Diplomacy/Yaalon-praises-Chuck-Hagel-as-true-friend-382736. Accessed April 6, 2019.

[74] Ibid.

[75] S.433- Iraq War De-Escalation Act of 2007, January 30, 2007, https://www.con gress.gov/bill/110th-congress/senate-bill/433/text. Accessed April 6, 2019.

CAP and CNAS, represented different thoughts within the liberal view. Second, Obama was one of few US Presidents who clearly recognized CAP's help to provide him with foreign policy staff and policy recommendations. However, this does not mean that there was a direct influence of CAP on Obama's foreign policy decision making. Last but not least, the fact that Obama recruited the president of the Atlantic Council, Chuck Hagel, to serve in his administration did not mean that this think tank might have had an influence on Obama's policies. This choice was attributed to Hagel's previous policy views on the Middle East when he was a US Republican senator as he harshly criticized Bush's foreign policy in the MENA area despite the fact that both Bush and Hagel belong to the same party.

Summary and Conclusion

This book discussed how some US non-state actors react, act, or pro-act in relation to issues pertaining to US foreign policy making in the MENA area. We analyzed how media, public opinion, interest groups, and think thanks interact with US Presidents' endeavors to sell their foreign policy ideas and decisions in the MENA region. The book's major aim was to find out whether the interaction between the aforementioned non-state actors and the executive power generates an impact from either direction. To put it differently, the book answered the following question: Who influences whom in US foreign policy to the Middle East and North Africa?

The first introductory chapter provided a concise synthesis of the conceptual and theoretical debate about the relationship between foreign policy making and the media, public opinion interest groups, and think tanks. We examined the role of these non-state players in initiating or shaping foreign policy in the Middle East and North Africa.

The section on the media highlighted the fact that there exists no full-fledged theory that explains a recognized causal impact of media on shaping policies in general. Therefore, we pointed out to two divergent and dominant scholarly directions that characterize the literature on the relationship between media and foreign policy making. The first line of thought is epitomized by the concept of the *CNN effect*. This line of thought defends the argument that the media, especially television, have a

© The Editor(s) (if applicable) and The Author(s), under exclusive license to Springer Nature Switzerland AG 2024
F. Touzani, *Marketing US Foreign Policy in the MENA Region*, Political Campaigning and Communication,
https://doi.org/10.1007/978-3-031-45143-0

152 SUMMARY AND CONCLUSION

significant impact on policymaking. On the other hand, the opponents of the CNN effect marginalize the influence of the media on policymaking. They argue that this understanding originated in humanitarian cases and any influence should be restricted to such cases. For instance, the constant exposure of pictures of a famine or a carnage by the media would prompt decision makers to act or react. Critics of the CNN effect postulate that the application of the *theory* on similar cases often yields contradictory findings. In addition to these prominent lines of thought, some scholars argue that the media's influence on policy making is contingent upon several factors including the political conditions in place and the nature of the problem under examination.

From a different vantage point, the media can be considered an *input* or an *output* variable. When the media are an input variable, they play the role of an influencer, which is explained by the theories of framing and agenda setting. However, when the media are considered an output variable, they are influenced by the policymakers, which is explained by the Media Management theory and the concept of "spin doctors".

The second section in the introductory chapter revolved around the scholarly debate on the relationship between the public opinion and foreign policy making with a focus on international critical issues such as wars or events that involve the use of force. The understanding of this relationship boils down to two different scholarly directions. The first is a realist approach. This approach minimizes the impactful role of public opinion in influencing US foreign policies owing to several factors. These include the fact that Americans tend to be a lot less interested in foreign policies unlike domestic ones because they think that these latter are directly related to their daily lives. Other factors include the public opinion's irrationality and the lack of reliable information about international critical issues. As a result, the public opinion are very likely to be manipulated by policymakers and, thus, follow their decisions.

The other approach is liberal. Proponents of this approach argue that the public opinion is at the center of foreign policy making. This can be attributed to the fact that policymakers have vested interests in satisfying the public opinion because they are behind their election and can affect their re-election. Therefore, the public opinion are very likely to play a constraining role, especially in liberal democracies such as the US.

The third section in the introductory chapter was about the conceptual and theoretical frameworks that explain the influential role of interest groups in policy making. The major conceptual framework views

SUMMARY AND CONCLUSION   153

the political influence of interest groups as a multi-stage process. The first stage requires interest groups to choose decisive lobbying tactics and strategies. For instance, an interest group may opt for grass-root campaigns to mobilize the public opinion to put pressure on policymakers. This may also include providing funds for presidential or congressional candidates to finance their electoral campaigns through the PACs.

The good use of such strategies enables interest groups to gain access to policymakers. Gaining access to policymakers is the second stage of the process of influence. The level of access depends on many factors such as the size of the interest group, its financial means as well as the leadership and the internal cohesion of the group. For instance, a large interest group with good financial resources is very likely to gain more access to policymakers. The multi-stage process of influence ends with the third stage whose major focus is to influence policies. Realizing an influence relies on the implementation of good lobbying tactics and the level of access to policymakers.

Theoretically speaking, we can differentiate between two main theories that explain the impactful role of interest groups on policymaking. Namely, pluralism and neo-corporatism. According to the pluralist perspective, politics and policymaking are a marketplace of competing ideas and ideologies which aim at grabbing the decision makers' attention in order to influence their decisions. In fact, this is a realistic understanding of the relationship between interest groups and policymakers. The fact that there is a competition between different ideas guarantees a balanced access to policymakers and prevents the monopoly of ideas. Consequently, the influence on policymaking is very likely to be regulated.

The corporatist theoretical perspective provides an institutional explanation of the relationship between interest groups and policymaking. Proponents of this view argue that policymaking is a process whose outcome is the product of institutional cooperation between interest groups and the government.

The last section in the introductory chapter discussed the political influence of think tanks. While some scholars recognize the key role of think tanks in influencing policies, others conceive differently. They argue that it is very difficult to measure a potential influence or establish a causal relationship between the policy recommendations of think tanks and the decisions of policy makers, which can be attributed to some methodological constraints. However, connections between policies of

154 SUMMARY AND CONCLUSION

think tanks and those in office can still be made using various types of indicators. These include but not limited to presence in the media, testimonies in Congress, book sales, government consultations in addition to the number of think tanks' staff who are appointed to serve in different positions in US administrations.

The major theoretical framework that guides research on the political impact of think tanks is John W. Kingdon's multiple-stream theory. According to the theory, the policy agenda is a process that constitutes of three streams. Think tanks play a significant role in all of these streams, which culminates in influencing policies. While the problem stream denotes the type of issue under review, the policy stream refers to the quality of research and ideas provided by think tanks. Finally, the political stream highlights the think tanks' staff who are singled out to work in various government departments and agencies.

In the second chapter of this book, we examined the role of US media in shaping US foreign policy in the Middle East and North Africa from the onset of the *war on terror* to the beginning of the *Arab Spring*. Our analyses of presidential rhetoric and media coverage of major events during this period led to the following conclusions.

To begin with, American Presidents were generally more successful in setting the US media's agenda pertaining to US foreign policy in the MENA area. The Presidents' effective use of the rhetoric of fear and democracy through well-crafted frames and propaganda campaigns compelled most US media to mirror their rhetoric and adopt their foreign policy agenda with minor criticism. This was clear in four case studies: The war in Iraq (2003), the intervention in Libya (2011), the Egyptian revolution (2011), and Iran's nuclear program (2001–2013).

Taking advantage of the feeling of fear that existed after September 11, George Bush fostered this feeling through constructing images of "threat" about Saddam Hussein's Iraq and Iran's nuclear program. The US intervention in Libya and the US response to the Egyptian uprising were driven by humanitarian and democratic concerns, which were successfully sold by Barack Obama. In these four cases, the US media played a very minor role and were mostly reflecting Bush's and Obama's rhetoric as their coverage was mainly relying on official sources.

On the other hand, the cases which involved a generally more important role of the US media are the following: First, the occupation of Iraq (2003–2013) which coincided with the disclosure of many facts and scandals including the absence of WMDs in Iraq, the US human rights abuses

SUMMARY AND CONCLUSION 155

at Abu Ghraib and Guantanamo prisons and the increase in human losses among American forces in Iraq. Second, there is the Benghazi attacks in 2012. These attacks resulted in murdering American diplomats and raised a huge controversy about Obama's responses to the attacks. Last but not least, there is Obama's suggestion of a US military intervention in Syria in 2013 after the use of chemical weapons.

A close look at these three cases reveals that the US media are more likely to play an important role in American foreign policy in the MENA area when the issues under discussion involve risking American lives and marring the image of the US as a democratic country that respects human rights. This conditioned important role is mainly related to shaping the public opinion about a particular foreign policy issue rather than setting the US foreign policy agenda. The only case which may illustrate the US media role in setting the US foreign policy agenda was deterring Obama from militarily intervening in Syria. However, it is not clear whether it was due to the media or due to the official opposition in Congress.

In sum, while we can safely say that the US media play a key role in raising Americans' awareness and shaping their opinion about issues in the MENA region, their role in setting the US foreign policy agenda in the region remains less significant.

Chapter III discussed the influential role of US public opinion in shaping US foreign policy in the MENA area. The analyses were carried out in the light of five presidencies from Ronald Reagan to Barack Obama. We examined the presidents' foreign policies with a focus on US military interventions in the MENA region along with the results of public opinion polls pertaining to critical issues that coincided with the same period. The chapter's major goal was to assess the US public opinion's ability to influence the Presidents' policies regarding the use of force.

The analyses of the five case studies revealed that the US public opinion played a very limited role in shaping US foreign policy in the MENA area, especially pertaining to the use of force in the region. This is mainly due to a very significant dominance of the executive power, which is in line with the realist thoughts about the role of public opinion in shaping foreign policy.

The marginalized role of the US public opinion is attributed to two major factors. First, American presidents might totally or partially ignore US public opinion because they believe that it is passionate and irrational. As a result, the public opinion's choice might not serve US national

156 SUMMARY AND CONCLUSION

interests. Second, the US public opinion can often be manipulated by presidential rhetoric through PR campaigns that aim at framing the issues under discussion in a specific manner to garner public support to use force. All in all, if the US public opinion does not support the Presidents' foreign policy plans, the Presidents are more likely to ignore it or try to manipulate it.

Chapter IV examined the following question: Why AIPAC succeeds or fails to shape US foreign policy in the Middle East and North Africa? Under which circumstances and using which strategies? We discussed this question during the presidencies of George W. Bush and Barack Obama within the contexts of the Palestinian-Israeli conflict and Iran nuclear program. Shaping foreign policies is a tri-stage process that starts with choosing the right strategies through which interest groups can gain access to policymakers, which might lead to influencing foreign policies.

As for the first stage, which deals with AIPAC's lobbying strategies, AIPAC tries to shape and dominate the public opinion in relation to US foreign policy in the MENA area through monitoring and influencing the media, keeping an eye on academia and winning the war of ideas in the world of Washington think tanks.

To monitor and influence the media, AIPAC relies on numerous pro-Israel journalists and reporters in addition to mobilizing the public opinion to put pressure on media outlets which report or broadcast news critical of Israel's policies in the Middle East or question US unconditional support to Israel. The lobbying tactics include urging its followers to send mass messages or make mass phone calls to media managers as well as boycott the media outlets or organize protests at their offices.

To control the academia, AIPAC targets students, faculty, and administrators. To influence students, AIPAC funds academic programs that endorse Israel, trains student leaders in Washington to influence their peers on campuses, invites heads of student governments to its Annual Policy Conference for participation and training, and offers internships for college students.

In addition to students, AIPAC monitors anti-Israel or anti-semitic practices among faculty members on campuses through urging students to report such practices via an online platform in its website. In addition, AIPAC incites its followers to coerce college administrators not to hire professors who are likely to be critical of Israel through sending mass messages and making mass phone calls. Finally, AIPAC is keen on funding and promoting academic programs on Israel studies.

SUMMARY AND CONCLUSION   157

To win the war of ideas in Washington, AIPAC establishes and funds pro-Israel think tanks that constitute of its former staff and funded by its donors such as the Washington Institute for Near East Policy (WINEP) and the Saban Center for Middle East Policy. This is in addition to maintaining a strong presence of pro-Israel staff in conservative think tanks in Washington.

In addition to shaping the public opinion through the media, academia, and think tanks, AIPAC has specific lobbying programs that directly target specific religious, ethnic, and business communities.

As for the second stage of influence, which deals with how AIPAC gains access to policymakers regarding US foreign policy in the MENA area, we differentiated between gaining access to members of Congress and Presidents or Presidential candidates. The general conclusion we drew is that it is easier for AIPAC to gain access to members of Congress than to Presidents.

AIPAC gains access to members of Congress through various means. First and foremost, AIPAC's related PACs and individual donors generously contribute to the campaigns of congressional candidates who are more likely to defend Israel's interests in Congress. Furthermore, AIPAC uses more direct means such as frequently meeting with members of Congress and their staffers, organizing briefings for them, sending copies of its monthly policy journal to congressional offices, drafting speeches and legislations, conducting research, organizing fully funded trips for members of Congress and their staffers to Israel, and inviting them to its Annual Policy Conference. This is in addition to urging its lobbyists to pressure legislators to vote for resolutions that serve Israel's interests and oppose those that do not through sending mass messages and making mass phone calls to their representatives in Congress.

AIPAC gains access to Presidents and Presidential candidates through several means. One of the major ones is the financial contributions to the presidential campaigns through the PACs and individuals affiliated with AIPAC. Moreover, AIPAC mobilizes the Jewish voters who have the highest turnout in the US and are concentrated in decisive states. Last but not least, AIPAC is very keen on having Jewish or pro-Israel individuals hold high positions in the Presidents' administrations.

As for the third stage, which deals with influencing US foreign policy pertaining to the Palestinian-Israeli conflict and the Iran nuclear program, we came to the following conclusions. The first general conclusion is that AIPAC remains a very strong interest group mainly because of its

158 SUMMARY AND CONCLUSION

comprehensive and pointed lobbying strategies that allow it to have a relatively easy access to policymakers. However, having access to policymakers does not always result in influencing their decisions in regard to the Palestinian-Israeli conflict and Iran nuclear program.

To begin with, we noted that AIPAC had more influence on Congress than on the Presidents regarding the selected issues, which can be attributed to several factors. First, AIPAC relies on reliable Jewish, Christian Zionist, and pro-Israel members of Congress. These members exhibit unconditional moral support for AIPAC's agenda. Second, there is much more money flowing into congressional campaigns than Presidential ones from AIPAC's affiliated PACs and individuals. Third, AIPAC does much better job mobilizing its lobbyists to put pressure on their congressional representatives than on Presidents. Finally, some international factors, such as UN resolutions or political changes in the MENA region, facilitate AIPAC's success in lobbying members of Congress.

As for the factors that influence AIPAC's low influence on Presidents, we mention the following: Initially, the image of the US in the region or its security interests may be undermined by what AIPAC advocates for. Additionally, the President may succeed in framing the issues under discussion in a way that allows him to garner the public support taking into consideration the public's negative experience with similar issues. In this case, it is very hard for AIPAC to influence the public opinion to think otherwise. Furthermore, we also noted a limitation in AIPAC's ability to influence the administration's appointments, which contributes in minimizing its overall influence on the President's foreign policy decisions in the region.

Chapter V discussed the impact of US think tanks on US Presidents' foreign policies in the MENA region using Kingdon's Multiple-Streams theory and focusing on three presidencies: Bill Clinton (1993–2001), George Bush (2001–2009), and Barrack Obama (2009–2017).

The first conclusion relates to the types of think tanks from which US Presidents recruit their foreign policy experts and the dominance of these experts in the Presidents' administrations. Clinton and Obama heavily relied on foreign policy experts from a combination of academic, contract, and advocacy think tanks. However, Bush predominantly relied on advocacy think tanks which advocate for conservative ideas. We noted that this choice has an impact on the Presidents' foreign policies, which was reflected in the difference between the foreign policies of Clinton, Bush, and Obama in the MENA area.

SUMMARY AND CONCLUSION   159

Additionally, unlike Clinton and Obama, whose foreign policy staff were mostly scholars in think tanks and did not serve in previous administrations, most of Bush's foreign policy staff served in previous administrations before joining think tanks. This suggests that American presidents can recruit their staff mainly because of their scholarly reputation and their affiliation with a particular think tank. On the other hand, Presidents can also recruit staff from specific think tanks not because of their affiliation with those think tanks. Rather, they appoint them due to their political experience serving in previous administrations or as members of Congress. This was the case with President Bush and most of PNAC founders in addition to Obama and Chuck Hagel.

The second conclusion relates to the strong connections that exist between think tanks' policy recommendations and foreign policy decisions of Clinton, Bush, and Obama in the MENA area. Nevertheless, these connections should not be understood as causal relationships for two main reasons. Initially, the alignment between the Presidents' foreign policy decisions and think tanks' policy recommendations cannot always be ascribed to the reputation of a particular think tank as an independent institution that aims at influencing policies through providing professional research. Bush and PNAC are a case in point. The Bush case study suggests that Bush adopted PNAC's policy recommendations because of the individuals who established it such as Dick Cheney and Donald Rumsfeld. These individuals were experienced politicians, not professional researchers, who served in previous Republican administrations, and whose neoconservative ideologies preceded the establishment of PNAC. Therefore, the establishment of PNAC was just an institutional medium through which these individuals could channel their political convictions.

Second, it is not clear whether the drastic change in Clinton's foreign policy in the MENA area was largely owing to the revolutionary victory of Republicans in Congress in 1994, or it was due to the strong pressure from well-known conservative think tanks such as the AEI or Heritage Foundation. All in all, the connections that may sometimes seem strong between policy recommendations of think tanks and US Presidents' foreign policies should not always be viewed as a direct impact of these think tanks on the Presidents' foreign policy decisions.

REFERENCES

"A Clean Break: A New Strategy for Securing the Realm". January 25, 2014. The Wayback Machine, Institute for Advanced Strategic and Political Studies. July, 2006.

Abelson, E. Donald. "Think Tanks in the United States". In Diane Stone, Andrew Denham, and Mark Garnett (Eds.), *Think Tanks Across Nations: A Comparative Approach*. Manchester University Press, 1998.

Abelson, Donald E. *A Capitol Idea: Think Tanks & Foreign Policy*. Quebec, Canada: McGillQueen's University Press, 2006.

Abelson E. Donald. *Do Think Tanks Matter? Assessing the Impact of Public Policy Institutes*. 2nd ed. I McGill-Queen's University Press, 2009.

Alden, Chris and Amnon Aran. *Foreign Policy Analysis: New Approaches*. Routledge, 2017.

Almond, Gabriel A. and G. Bingham Powell, Jr. *Comparative Politics Today: A World View*. Boston, 1980.

Almond, Gabriel, Bingham Powell, Aare Strom and R. J. Dalton. *Comparative Politics Today: A World View*. Singapore Pearson Education, Inc, 2000.

Bachner, Jennifer and Benjamin Ginsberg. *America's State Governments: A Critical Look at Disconnected Democracies*. Routledge, 2020.

Baker, A. James III. *The Politics of Diplomacy: Revolution, War, and Peace*, 1989–1992. New York: Putnam, 1995.

Bard, Mitchell G. "Tenured or Tenuous: Defining the Role of Faculty in Supporting Israel on Campus". The Israel on Campus Coalition and the American-Israeli Cooperative Enterprise. May 2004.

© The Editor(s) (if applicable) and The Author(s), under exclusive license to Springer Nature Switzerland AG 2024
F. Touzani, *Marketing US Foreign Policy in the MENA Region*, Political Campaigning and Communication,
https://doi.org/10.1007/978-3-031-45143-0

162 REFERENCES

Baroni, Laura, Brendan Carroll and Adam William Chalmers et al, "Defining and Classifying Interest Groups". Interest Groups & Advocacy 3 (2014): 149–151.

Bennett, Lance W. "Toward a Theory of Press-State Relations in the United States". *Journal of Communication* 40 (2) (1990): 103–25.

Bennett, Lance, Regina G. Lawrence, and Steven Livingston. *When the Press Fails: Political Power and the News Media From Iraq to Katrina.* Chicago: University of Chicago Press, 2008.

Bentham, Jeremy. *Works of Jeremy Bentham.* New York: Russell and Russell, 1962.

Bernhagen, Patrick. "Who Gets What in British Politics—And How? An Analysis of Media Reports on Lobbying Around Government Policies, 2001–7". Political Studies, 2011.

Besser, James D. "Turning Up Heat in Campus Wars". Jewish Week. July 25, 2003.

Beyers, Jan. "Gaining and Seeking Access: The European Adaptation of Domestic Interest Associations". European Journal of Political Research (2002): 585–612.

Beyers, Jan and Caelesta Braun. "Ties That Count: Explaining Interest Group Access to Policy Makers". Journal of Public Policy 34 (1) (2014): 93–121.

Biale, David. *Power and Powerlessness in Jewish History.* New York: Schocken Books, 1986.

Birnbaum, Jefferey H. "Washington's Poser 25". Fortune. December 8, 1997.

Blondel, Jean. *Comparative Government: A Reader.* Garden City, NY: Anchor Books, 1969.

Bouwen, Pieter. "Corporate Lobbying: Towards a Theory of Access". Journal of European Public Policy (2002): 365–390.

Breuning, Marijke. *Foreign Policy Analysis: A Comparative Introduction.* Springer, 2007.

Burchill, Scott. In "Liberalism". Scott Burchill, et al. (Eds.), *Theories of International Relations*, Fourth Edition. New York: Palgrave Macmillan, 2009.

Bush, George. "A Gulf War Exclusive: President Bush Talking with David Frost". Journal Graphics, 1996.

Byman, Daniel and Sara Bjerg Miller. "Thé United States and the Middle East: Interest, Risks and Risks". Sustainable Security, 2016, p. 263n. DOI:https://doi.org/10.1093/acprof:oso/9780190611477.003.0011

Campbell, Kurt, and Michele Flournoy. "To Prevail: An American Strategy for the Campaign Against Terrorism". CSIS Significant Issues Series. CSIS, November, 2001.

Campbell, Kurt and Michele Flournoy. "The Intermittence and the Way Forward". Center for New American Security, 2007.

REFERENCES 163

Cannon, Lou. *President Reagan: The Role of a Lifetime*. New York: Simon & Schuster, 1991.

Carlsnaes, Walter, Thomas Risse and Beth A. Simmons. *Handbook of International Relations*. Sage, 2012.

Chan, Steve and William Safran. "Public Opinion as a Constraint against War: Democracies' Responses to Operation Iraqi Freedom". *Foreign Policy Analysis*, 2006.

Chandler, David. *From Kosovo to Kabul and Beyond: Human Rights and International Intervention*. London: Pluto Press, 2005.

Chari, Raj, John Hogan, Gary Murphy and Michele Crepaz. *Regulating Lobbying: A Global Comparison*. Manchester University Press, 2019.

Cheney, Richard B. In *My Time: A. Personal and Political Memoir*. New York, NY: Threshold Editions, 2011.

Clinton, Bill. "State of the Union Address", Speech, The American Presidency Project. University of California.

Cohen, Bernard. *The Press and Foreign Policy*. Princeton University Press, 1963.

Cohen, Yoel. *Media Diplomacy: The Foreign Office in the Mass Communications Age*. London: Frank Cass and Company Ltd, 1986.

Cohen, Richard E. and Peter Bell. "Congressional Insiders Poll". National Journal. March 5, 2005.

Cook, Timothy. *Governing with the News:The News Media as a Political Institution*. Chicago: University of Chicago Press, 1998.

Dahl, Robert. *Who Governs? Democracy and Power in an American City*. Yale University Press, 2005.

Diane, Stone. *Capturing the Political Imagination: Think Tanks and the Policy Process*. London: Frank Cass, 1996.

DiMaggio, Anthony. *Mass Media, Mass Propaganda: Examining American News in the "War on Terror."* Lanham, MD: Lexington Books, 2008.

DiMaggion, R. Anthony. *When Media Goes to War: Hegemonic Discourse, Public Opinion, and the Limits of Dissent*. New York: Monthly Review Press, 2009.

Domke, David. *God Willing? Political Fundamentalism in the White House, the "War on Terror" and the Echoing Press*. London: Pluto Press, 2004.

Dür, Andreas. "Measuring Interest Group Influence in the EU: A Note on Methodology". European Union Politics, 2008.

Duverger, Maurice. *Party Politics and Pressure Groups*. Thomas Nelson & Sons Ltd, 1972.

Feist, Samuel. "Facing Down the Global Village: The Media Impact". In R. L. Kugier and E. Frost, *The Global Century*, pp. 709–725. Washington, DC: National Defense University Press, 2001.

Finnegan, Lisa. *No Questions Asked: News Coverage since 9/11*. Westport, CT: Praeger, 2006.

164 REFERENCES

Foyle, Douglas C. *Counting the Public in: Presidents, Public opinion and Foreign Policy.* Columbia University Press, 1999.

Frankel, Glenn. "Hussein Denies Charges in Interview Oil Is U.S. Goal, Iraqi Leader Says". *Washington Post*, February 5, 2003. A17.

Franssen, Herman. "Obama and Declining US Dependence on Imported Oil and Gas". Middle East Institute, 2014.

Gehlen, Martin. Politikberafung in den USA. Der Einflub Der Think Tanks AUI die amerikanische Sozialpolitik. Frankfurt, 2005.

Geraphty, J. Timothy. *Peacekeeping at War: Beirut 1983—The Marine Commander Tells His Story.* Sterling, VA: Potomac Books, 2009.

Gilboa, Eytan. "The CNN Effect: The Search for a Communication Theory of International Relations". *Political Communication* 22 (2005): 27–44.

Goodman, Melvin. *Failure of Intelligence: The Decline and Fall of the CIA.* Lanham, MD: Rowman & Littlefield, 2008.

Gowing, Nik. "Real-Time Television Coverage of Armed Conflicts and Diplomatic Crises: Does It Pressure or Distort Foreign Policy Decisions?" Working Paper 94–1, Joan Shorenstein Barone Center on the Press, Politics and Public Policy, John F. Kennedy School of Government, Harvard University, June, 1994.

Green, Mark, and Michele Jolin (Ed.). *Change for America: A Progressive Blueprint for the 44th President.* Basic Books, 2009.

Groshek, Christopher. "Shifting Dissent: Media Coverage of the Decision to Go to War in Iraq". International Communication Association Conference, New York, 2005.

Hamilton, Alexander, John Jay and James Madison. *The Federalist.* New York: Modern Library, 1983.

Hammond, Philip. *Framing Post-Cold War Conflicts: The Media and International Intervention.* Manchester: Manchester University Press, 2007.

Hannity Sean, and Alan Colmes. "Interview with Neil Dobro, Steven Zunes". Fox News, February 17, 2003, 9 p.m.

Han, Hahrie, Kenneth T. Andrews, Marshall Ganz, Matthew Baggetta, and Chaeyoon Lim. 2011. "The Relationship of Leadership Quality to the Political Presence of Civic Associations". Perspectives on Politics 9 (1) (2011): 45–59.

Hayes, Chris. "All In with Chris Hayes". MSNBC, June 14, 2013, 8 p.m. est.

Hill, Christopher. *The Changing Politics of Foreign Policy.* Palgrave, 2003.

Hitchner Dell and Carole Levine. *Comparative Government and Politics.* New York, Dodd Mead & Co, 1967.

Holsti, R. Ole. *Public Opinion and American Foreign Policy.* Ann Arbor, MI: University of Michigan Press, 1996.

REFERENCES 165

IBP USA. *Israel Lobby in the United States Handbook: Volume 1 Strategic Information, Organization, Operations, Performance.* USA International Business Publications, 2018.

Indyk, Martin S., Kenneth G. Lieberthal and Michael E. O'Hanlon. *Bending History: Barack Obama's Foreign Policy.* Brookings Institution Press, 2012.

Iyengar, Shanto and Adam Simon. "News Coverage of the Gulf Crisis and Public Opinion". In W. Lance Bennett and David L. Paletz, *Taken by Storm: The Media, Public Opinion, and US Foreign Policy in the Gulf War*, 167–186. Chicago: Chicago University Press, 1994.

Jackson, Richard. *Writing the War on Terrorism: Language, Politics and Counter-Terrorism.* Manchester: Manchester University Press, 2006.

Jasperson, Amy, and Mansour O. El-Kikhia. "CNN and al Jazeera's Media Coverage of America's War in Afghanistan". In *Framing Terrorism, Norris, Kern, and Just* (2004): 113–132.

Jett, Dennis. *The Iran Nuclear Deal: Bombs, Bureaucrats, and Billionaires.* Springer, 2018.

Jentleson, W. Bruce. *American Foreign Policy: The Dynamics of Choice in the 21st Century.* W. W. Norton.

Kant, Immanuel. *Perpetual Peace, and Other Essays on Politics, History, and Morals.* Indianapolis: Hackett, 1983. Introduced and translated by Ted Humphrey.

Katz, S. Richard. Politische Partein in den Vereinigten States. Fokus Amerika Der Friedrich- Ebert-Stiftung. Washington DC, 2007.

Kegley, Charles W. *World Politics: Trend and Transformation.* Wadsworth Publishing 12th Edition, 2008.

Kessler, Jonathan S., and Jeff Schwaber. The AIPAC College Guide: Exposing the Anti-Israel Campaign on Campus; AIPAC Papers on U.S.-Israel Relations. American Israel Public Affairs Committee, 1984.

Kingdon, W. John. *Agendas, Alternatives, and Public Policies.* Boston: Little Brown, 2010.

Koppel, Ted. "Crisis Coverage and the Candy Bar Imperative". In *Feet to the Fire: The Media After 9/11*, ed. Kristina Borjesson. Amherst, NY: Prometheus Books, 2005.

Ladi, Stella. *Globalization, Policy Transfer and Policy Research Institutes.* Edward Elgar Publishing, 2005.

Laipson, Ellen. "Think Tanks: Supporting Cast Players in the National Security Enterprise". In George Roger and Harry Rishikof (Eds.), *The National Security Enterprise: Navigating the Labyrinth.* Washington, DC: Georgetown University Press.

Lake, Anthony. *The Vietnam Legacy: The War, American Society and the Future of American Foreign Policy.* New York: New York University Press, 1976.

166 REFERENCES

Lawrence Regina G., Steven Livingston and Lance W. Bennett. *When the Press Fails: Political Power and the News Media From Katrina to Iraq*. Chicago: Chicago University Press, 2007.

Lippmann, Walter. *Essays in the Public Philosophy*. Boston: Little, Brown and Company, 1955.

Livingston, Samuel and Todd Eachus. "Humanitarian Crises and U.S. Foreign Policy: Somalia and the CNN Effect Reconsidered". *Political Communication* 12 (1995): 413–429.

Livingston, Samuel. "Clarifying the CNN Effect: An Examination of Media Effects According to Type of Military Intervention". Research Paper R-18, June, Cambridge, MA: The Joan Shorenstein Barone Center on the Press. Politics and Public Policy at Harvard University, 1997.

Lowi, Theodore. *The End of Liberalism: The Second Republic of the United States*. W. W. Norton & Company, 2009.

Mann, James. *The Rise of the Vulcans: The History of Bush's War Cabinet*. New York, NY: Penguin Group, 2004.

Mann, James. *The Obamians: The Struggle Inside the White House to Redefine American Power*. New York, NY: Penguin Group, 2012.

Mansour, Camille. *Beyond Alliance: Israel in U.S. Foreign Policy*. Translated by James A. Cohen. NewYork: Columbia University Press, 1994.

McCombs, Maxwell and Amy Reynolds. "News Influence on Our Pictures of the World". *Media Effects* (2002): 11–28.

McCormick, M. James. *American Foreign Policy & Process*. Cengage Learning, 2013.

McGann, J. G. and R. K. Weaver (Eds.). *Think Tanks and Civil Societies: Catalysts for Ideas and Action*. London: Transaction Publishers, 2000.

McGann, James G. *Think Tanks and Policy Advice in the United States: Academics, Advisors and Advocates*. Abingdon, UK: Routledge, 2007.

McTernan, John P. *As America Has Done to Israel*. Whitaker House, 2008.

Mearsheimer, John J. and Stephen M. Walt. *The Israel'Lobby and US Foreign Policy*. Farrar, Straus, and Giroux, 2007.

Mermin, Jonathan. "Television News and American Intervention in Somalia: The Myth of a Media-Driven Foreign Policy." *Political Science Quarterly* 12 (3) (1997): Fall.

Michalowitz, Irina. "Assessing Conditions for Influence of Interest Groups in the EU". IHS Political Science Series: 2005, 106.

Mitchell, Thomas G. *Israel /Palestine and the Politics of a Two-State Future*. McFarland, 2013.

Monroe. D, Alan. "Public Opinion and Public Policy: 1980–1993". Public Opinion Quarterly 62 (1) (May) 1998, 6–28. https://doi.org/10.1086/297828

REFERENCES   167

Morin, Jean-Frédéric and Jonathan Paquin. *Foreign Policy Analysis: A Toolbox.* Springer, 2018.

Mueller, John E. *Policy and Opinion in the Gulf War.* Chicago: University of Chicago Press, 1994.

Natsios, Andrew. "Illusions of Influence: The CNN Effect in Complex Emergencies". In Robert I. Rotberg and Thomas G. Weiss (Eds.), *From Massacres to Genocide: The Media, Public Policy, and Humanitarian Crises.* Washington, DC: The Brookings Institute, 1996.

Neack, Laura. *The New Foreign Policy.* Maryland: Rowman & Littlefield Publishers, 2008.

Naveh, Chanan. "The Role of Media in Foreign Policy Decision Making: A Theoretical Framework." Conflict and Communication 1 (2): 2002.

Ned Lebow, Richard and Nathan Funk (Eds). *Richard Ned Lebow: A Pioneer in International Relations Theory, History, Political Philosophy and Psychology.* Springer, 2017.

Newsom, David D. *The Public Dimension of Foreign Policy.* Bloomington, IN: Indiana University Press, 1996.

Öberg, PerOla, Torsten Svensson, Peter Munk Christiansen, Asbjø Sonne Nørgaard, Hillary Rommetvedt and Gunnar Thesen. "Disrupted Exchange and Declining Corporatism: Government Authority and Interest Group Capability in Scandinavia". Government and Opposition (2001) 46 (3): 365–391.

Page, Benjamin I, and Robert Y. Shapiro. *The Rational Public: Fifty Years of Trends in Americans' Policy Preferences.* Chicago: University of Chicago Press, 1992.

Parsi, Trita. *Losing an Enemy: Obama, Iran and the Triumph of Diplomacy.* New Haven & London: Yale University Press, 2017.

Pfetsch, Barbara. "Government News Management". In *The Politics of News, The News of Politics.* CQ Press, 1998.

Political-media Effects on Public Opinion of War on Terror. November 2001-January 2002. Pew Research Center.

Powlick, J. Philip. "Foreign Policy Decisions and Public Opinion: The Case of the Lebanon Intervention, 1982–1984". American Political Science Association, Washington, DC, September 1, 1988.

"Progressive Internationalism: A Democratic National Security Strategy". Progressive Public Institute. October 30, 2003.

Ryan, Michael. "Framing the War against Terrorism: U.S. Newspaper Editorials and Military Action in Afghanistan". *International Communication Gazette* 66 (2004): 363–382.

Reagan, Ronald. "News Conference of December 20". Department of State Bulletin 84 (1984):7–8.

Reagan, Ronald. *An American Life.* New York: Simon & Schuster, 1990.

168 REFERENCES

Ricci, Davi. *The Transformation of American Politics: The New Washington and the Rise of Think Tanks*. Yale University Press, 1993.

Robinson, Piers. "The Policy-Media Interaction Model: Measuring Media Power During Humanitarian Crisis". *Journal of Peace Research* 37 (5) (2000): 613–633.

Robinson, Piers. *The CNN Effect: The Myth of News, Foreign Policy and Intervention*, 63–71. New York and London; Routledge, 2002.

Rojecki, Andrew. "Rhetorical Alchemy: American Exceptionalism and the War on Terror". Political Communication 25 (2008): 67–88.

Ross, Dennis. *Doomed to Succeed: The US-Israel Relationship from Truman to Obama*. McMillan, 2015.

Ruebner, Josh. *Shattered Hopes: Obama's Failure to Broker Israeli-Palestinian Peace*. New York: Verso, 2014.

Schorr, Daniel. " CNN Effect: Edge-of-seat Diplomacy". *Christian Science Monitor* 27: (1998): 11.

Said, Edward. *Orientalism*. New York: Vintage, 1979.

Said, Edward. *Covering Islam: How the Media and the Experts Determine How We See the Rest of the World*. New York: Vintage, 1997.

Schultz, Ed. "The Ed Show". MSNBC, May 12, 2013, 5 p.m. est.

Singer, David and Lawrence Grossman. American Jewish Year Book 2002. *American Jewish Committee*: Springer, Vol. 102, 2003.

Smith, Steve, Amelia Hadfield, and Tim Dunne. *Foreign Policy: Theories, Actors, Cases*. Oxford University Press, 2016.

Sterling-Folker, Jennifer. "Between a Rock and a Hard Place. Assertive and Post Cold-War US Foreign Policy". James M. Scott (Ed.) *After the End. Making US Foreign Policy in the Post-Cold-War World*. Durham: Duke University Press, 1998.

Stone, Diane. "Introduction. Think Tanks, Policy Advice and Governance". In Diane Stone and Andrew Denham (Eds.): *Think Tanks Traditions, Policy Research, and Politics of Ideas*. Manchester University Press, 2004.

Tocqueville, Alexis de. *Democracy in America*. New York: Vintage, 1958.

Truman, David. *The Governmental Process Political Interests and Public Opinion*. New York Alfred A Knopf, 1951.

Waltz, Kenneth. *Theory of International Politics*. Reading, MA: Addison-Wesley Publication 1979.

Wittkopf, R. Eugene and Christopher M. Jones. *American Foreign Policy: Pattern and Process* New York: St Martin's press, 2012, p. 265.

Wolfsfeld, Gadi. *Media and Political Conflict: News from the Middle East*. Cambridge University Press, 1997.

Woodward, Bob. *The Commanders*. New York: Simon & Schuster, 1991.

REFERENCES 169

Zaller, John. "Strategic Politicians, Public Opinion and the Gulf Crisis". In W. Lance Bennett and David L. Paletz (Eds.), *Taken by Storm*. Chicago: University of Chicago Press, 1994.

Index

A
Abbas, Mahmoud, 104
Abelson, E. Donald, 21
Abrams, Elliott, 140
Abu Ghraib prison, 41
Academic think tanks, 127
Action Center, 96
Acts of war, 26
Advocacy think tanks, 128
Agenda-setting theory, 12
Ahmedinejad, Mahmoud, 45
AIPAC's lobbying strategies, 87
Al Assad, Bashar, 59
Albright, Madeline, 131
Almond, Gabriel, 83, 84
Alterman, Eric, 88
American Enterprise Institute (AEI), 134, 137
American Friends of Likud (AFL), 119
American Israel Education Foundation (AIEF), 95
American Israel Public Affairs Committee (AIPAC), 86

A New Beginning, 147
Anomic groups, 84
Anti-Semitism, 87
Arab League, 104
Arab Spring, 11
Arafat, 104
Assertive multilateralism, 133
Associational groups, 85
Axis of evil, 45

B
Baker, James, 71
Behavioral approaches, 5
Beirut attacks, 69
Benghazi, 57
Bennett, Lance W., 10
Bentham, Jeremy, 15
Berman, Howard, 109
Biological weapons, 31
Body-bag Effect, 10
Bolton, John, 141
Book sales, 22
Briefing Book, 95
Brookings Institution, 90, 127

© The Editor(s) (if applicable) and The Author(s), under exclusive license to Springer Nature Switzerland AG 2024
F. Touzani, *Marketing US Foreign Policy in the MENA Region*, Political Campaigning and Communication,
https://doi.org/10.1007/978-3-031-45143-0

172 INDEX

Bush administration, 33
Bush, George H. W., 70
Bush, George W., 74
Business interest groups, 85

C
Campbell, Kurt, 145
Campus Watch, 91
Cardin, Benjamin, 110
Carnegie Corporation, 132
Carnegie Endowment for
International Peace (CEIP), 140
Cato Institute, 140
Causal influence, 8
Ceasefire, 67
Center for National Policy (CNP),
131
Center for New American Security
(CNAS), 145
Center for Responsive Politics (CRP),
94
Center for Security Policy (CSP), 137
Center for Strategic and International
Studies (CSIS), 131
Center of American Progress (CAP),
143
Checks and balances, 22, 62
Cheney, Dick, 137
Christians United for Israel (CUFI),
86
Citizens interest groups, 85
Clash of civilizations, 52
Clinton, Bill, 73
CNN Effect, 9
Cognitive school, 6
Cohen, Bernard, 12
Cole, Jonathan, 92
Commander-in-chief, 79
Congressional testimonies, 22
Contemporary approaches, 5
Contract think tanks, 128

Cosmetic policy, 10
Council on American Islamic
Relations (CAIR), 86
Council on Foreign Relations (CFR),
131
Critical events, 39

D
Defensive measures, 27
DeLay, Tom, 101, 102
Democratic Leadership Council
(DLC), 130
Discourse of democracy, 50

E
Egyptian Revolution, 52
Elbaradei, Mohamed, 49
Elitist theory, 20
Enemy, 26
Enemy combatants, 43
Epistemic communities, 7
Evenhandedness, 106
ExxonMobil, 86

F
Fear, 26
Federalist Papers, 16
Feith, Douglas, 141
Flournoy, Michele, 145
Foreign corporations, 56
Foreign policy making, 3
Fortune magazine, 86
Founding fathers, 16
416Labs, 88
Fox News, 49
Frame, 12
Framing, 12
Friedman, Howard, 94
Fuel swap, 115

INDEX 173

G
Gaddafi's regime, 77
Gaddafi, Muammar, 55
Gaining access, 18
Gatestone Institute, 141
Geneva conventions, 43
Global media, 11
Global order, 34
Grant, 84
Guantanamo Bay, 41

H
Hagee, John, 112
Hagel, Chuck, 107, 148
Heritage Foundation, 133
High risk, 10
Hitchner, Dell, 84
Hoover Institution, 136
Hostile regime, 28
Hot pursue, 142
Hudson Institute, 141
Humanitarian crisis, 9
Hunter, Robert, 131
Hussein, Saddam, 32, 70

I
Idealism, 4
Identity groups, 85
Impact indicators, 23
Impeachment, 74
Indexing theory, 11
Indicators, types of, 22
Indyk, Martin, 90, 97
Input variable, 11
Institute for Zionist Strategies (IZS),
142
Institutional groups, 85
Interest groups, 17
Internal cohesion, 19
International Atomic Energy Agency's
(IAEA), 113

International Criminal Court (ICC),
109
Intervention in Somalia, 9
Intifada, 91
Iran, 45
Iraqi oil, 70
Iraq Liberation Act, 135
Iraq Study Group (ISG), 33
Irrationality, 15

J
Joint Comprehensive Plan Of Action
(JCPOA), 118
Jordan, Eason, 88

K
Kant, Immanuel, 15
Kay, David, 39
Khalidi, Rashid, 92
Kingdon, John W., 23
Kohr, Howard, 120
Kuwait, 70

L
Lake, Anthony, 131
Lantos, Tom, 114
Lebanon, 67
Levine, Carole, 84
Libby, Scooter, 142
Liberal approach, 14
Libyan uprising, 55
Libya's oil, 78
Lieberman, Joseph, 102
Lobbies, 83
Lobbying, 83
Lobbying technique, 18
Lott, Trent, 101

M
MacArthur Foundation, 132

174 INDEX

Mandate for Change, 130
Massing, Michael, 89
McCombs, Max, 12
McGann, James G., 22
Mearsheimer, John, 140
Media discourse, 28
Media management (MM), 12
Media pressure, 10
Menendez, Robert, 119
Military intervention, 27
Mitchell, George, 105
Morsi, Mohammed, 54
Mubarak's regime, 52
Multiple-Streams theory, 23
Multi-stage process, 17

N
Nagl, John, 145
National Association of Arab
    Americans (NAAA), 86
NATO, 55
Near East Report, 95
Neo-corporatism, 19
Neo-corporatist theory, 20
Netanyahu, Benjamin, 110
News networks, 11
Newspaper editorials., 28
New Yorker, 41
New York Times, The, 35
No-fly zone, 55
Non-associational groups, 85
Non-coercive, 11
Nuclear weapons, 31

O
Obama's rhetoric, 79
Obamians, The, 143
Official rhetoric, 38
Olmert, Ehud, 104
Open Society Foundations, 132
Operation Desert Storm, 72

Operation Desert Strike, 135
Operation Restore Hope, 9
Opinion polls, 14
Opposite directions, 10
Orientalist discourse, 52
Oslo accords, 91
Output indicators, 23
Output variable, 12

P
Palestinian Statehood Bid, 110
Party discipline, 126
Party think tanks, 130
Peacekeeping, 67
Peace Now, 107
Perle, Richard, 142
Petraeus, David, 145
Pluralism, 19
Pluralist theory, 19
Podesta, John, 144
Policy agenda, 23
Policy Conference, 96
Policy Stream, 23
Political Action Committees (PACs),
    18
Political circumstances, 10
Political reforms, 50
Political Stream, 24
Post-9/11 era, 26
Powell, Bingham, 84
Presidential framing, 28
Presidential propaganda, 33
Presidential rhetoric, 28
Pressure groups, 83
Problem Stream, 23
Progressive Policy Institute (PPI), 130
Project for the New American
    Century (PNAC), 134
Public agenda, 12
Public interest groups, 85
Public relations (PR) campaigns, 12

R

RAND Corporation, 128
Rational Actor Model, 6
Rational-choice theory, 4
Reagan, Ronald, 67
Realism, 4
Realist approach, 15
Red line, 61
Regime change, 48
Republican Revolution, 133
Resolution 1929, 116
Resolution 2334, 108
Resolutions 661, 133
Resource indicators, 22
Rhetoric of fear, 27
Ricci, David, 21
Rice, Condoleezza, 105
Rice, Susan, 147
Road Map, 102
Rogue state, 135
Ross, Dennis, 97, 106
Rumsfeld, Donald, 137

S

Saban Center, 90
Saban, Haim, 90
Said, Edward, 92
Salience, 12
Schorr, Daniel, 9
Security Council, 72
Security fence, 103
Self-interest, 4
Separation barrier, 103
Shalev, Menachem, 89
Sharon, Ariel, 91
Soviet expansion, 69
Soviet Union, 55
Spin concept, 12
Spin doctors, 13
Statement of Principles, 134
Stevens, Christopher, 58
Stone, Diane, 21

Strategies and tactics, 17
Streams, 23

T

Tactical policy, 10
Tactics of terror, 27
Talbott, Strobe, 132
Terrorism, 28
Tocqueville, Alexis de, 16
Traditional approaches, 4
Truman, David, 83
TV coverage, 28

U

United Nations Special Commission
   (UNSCOM), 73
Universities without students, 127
Urban Institute, 128
US Marine, 68
Utilization indicators, 22

V

Veto, 109
Vulcans, 136

W

Walt, Stephen M., 140
War of ideas, 89, 130
War on terror, 11, 26
Washington Institute, 90
Washington Institute for Near East
   Policy (WINEP), 90
Washington Post, The, 34
Weak party order, 22
Weapons of Mass Destruction
   (WMDs), 30
Weinberg, Barbi, 90
Weinberg, Larry, 90
Wikileaks, 11
Wurmser, David, 142